THE BEST NEW CR

CW00347632

The Ne

VOLUME THREE

Unlimited Overs

EDITED BY ROB STEEN

MAINSTREAM
PUBLISHING

EDINBURGH AND LONDON

First published in Great Britain in 1999 by
MAINSTREAM PUBLISHING COMPANY (EDINBURGH) LTD
7 Albany Street
Edinburgh EH1 3UG

ISBN 1 84018 238 5

Book design by Lance Bellers
Cover Photograph PA News

Printed and bound by Biddles Ltd

Contents

Editor's Note

Mixed emotions? They'd been stirred, scrambled, tossed and rammed in a blender. What emerged bore an uncomfortable resemblance to week-old chopped liver.

Six-fifteen am, the morning after *the* match. Or perhaps that should be the *match*: Australia–South Africa, World Cup semi-final. The buzz that had gripped me on the drive home from Edgbaston was still in residence. It is not every day, after all, that one attends the most exhilarating theatrical performance one could possibly wish to see. Hence the breathless yammering that had carried on in car, service station and Burger King for the thick end of four hours as Mike Marqusee, Huw Richards, Alastair McLellan and myself wended Smoke-wards, giddy with boyish wonder. But now the buzz was being yanked by the lapels and dragged towards the door.

Upon my return to Ally Pally, I had been greeted by my mother and sister: hardly the most frequent of welcoming committees – one resides in Poole, the other in Vienna (Virginia USA version). Throw in a wife similarly impervious to the allure of bat and ball, not to mention three sleeping children and a semi-comatose cocker spaniel, and the return to terra firma was as sudden and brutal as a cold shower during a hot date. Cruelly so seven hours later, when mother (even though they'd been divorced since Massie's Match) took the fateful phone call. Daddy, the Glaswegian George Castanza, had died in his sleep.

The possibility was there. Body and mind had been giving up, bit by bit, for some months, ever since the sour end to that memorable last fling in Cyprus (well, it was his third broken engagement in 12 weeks to an east European lass 40-odd years his junior). We just hadn't expected it so soon. My last conversation with him had been conducted under less-than ideal circumstances: me not-so-discreetly blubbing on the steps at the press box end of the Racecourse Ground just prior to the start of the final day of the Derby-Yorkie championship match, him almost speechless at the other end as he lay on his temporary bed in the psychiatric ward. I'd told him I'd understand if he'd had enough, if he no longer felt it was worth the struggle. For the first time since my barmitzvah, I spoke and he listened. Loving as we were, we always were an oddish couple.

Guilt, seldom a stranger, hammered hard and long. Jane whipped herself for missing his 70th birthday, for not saying goodbye. While Daddy was enduring his last day on this particular mortal coil, I had been immersing myself in flannelled frippery. Granted, I also happened to be earning a living, however self-indulgently, but that was no consolation. That cat 'o nine tails was working overtime. Fortunately, nothing had been left unsaid.

Then it dawned. Had the Berlin Philharmonic been in town, or Alfred Brendel, or his great chum Vladimir Ashkenazy, he would have done precisely the same. Without the slightest compunction (let alone a hundred-quid-plus-exes sweetener). Or so I convinced myself. When it came to the angst of composing a funeral address, I found myself comparing what he and my mother, respectively, had taught Jane and I. The maternal contribution came quickly enough: she had steeled us in the arts of survival. It took a great deal more pondering before I realised what he had instilled and nurtured: the capacity to experience joy, and express it. How apt that his fading hours should find his son doing just that. Cricket left him colder than an eskimo's extremities at a streaking festival, but I still suspect he is looking down at me now, nodding his forgiveness. Or so I've convinced myself.

IN WOODY ALLEN'S *Crimes and Misdemeanours*, Sharon relates how her great aunt May rejected the Bible because of its "unbelievable central character". Now the dust has settled, I feel much the same about Edgbaston '99 – on two counts. In the blond corner, Shane Warne, diminished by injury, usurped as his country's premier Test spinner and making what was predicted as his final bow on Pommy soil, yet delivering (with all due respect to that nice Mr Akhtar) the ball of the tournament before turning stroll into stagger. In the green corner, Lance Klusener, the fellow with the edgeless bat and nerves of purest tungsten, freezing when shit confronted fan. In the immortal words of Top Cat (though it may have been one of the Rugrats), who'd 'a thunk it?

What did the cockles to a crisp, though, was the realisation that we had just witnessed three hours of the most intense drama imaginable. From the moment Warney bamboozled Gibbs until that tragi-comic denouement, here was the apogee of the competitive arts. For those sweet three hours we lost ourselves, crowd and hacks alike, in a production scored by Bernstein, plotted by Hitchcock, staged by De Mille and animated by Chuck Jones. If it's got that swing, five days or one, who gives a XXXX?

In aesthetic terms, the two-act sketch, it scarce needs pointing out, will never be, can never be, a true match for the five-day play, but that doesn't mean it should always take a left turn off Quality Street and head straight for Slapstick Avenue. As the likes of South Park, The Simpsons and The Rugrats have demonstrated, cartoons can stimulate something other than funnybones. Dare we anticipate an end to the snobbery that has so consistently undermined England's limited-overs endeavours? Maybe, just maybe.

The seventh World Cup was far from flaw-free yet the overall impact was unquestionably beneficial. Surely the ICC would be better off staging the event more often – every other year at least – than sanctioning all those Pepsi-Fanta-Big Mac Triangulars. That way, in addition to reducing the opportunities for players and gamblers to consort, the show could return more frequently to Britain (all right pedants, Europe). Balls ducking and diving as if stitched by Arthur Daley and calibrated by Del Boy? Pish. Insufficient close finishes? That's akin, surely, to complaining about a shortage of multiple orgasms. For once, hallelujah, a one-day tourney found willow and cork reasonably evenly matched. Do away with those daft restrictions on the number of overs a chap can serve up and we really will have a game to reckon with.

THE NEW BALL VOLUME 3, not unnaturally, focuses primarily on the events of May and June. Framed by Tom Jenkins' vivid gallery, Brian Matthews takes guard first, roaming the murky waters of sport and nationalism, likening Australia's triumph to a Republican rallying-cry; Kevin Mitchell picks his way through the minefields of gambling and Pakistani cricket with characteristic insight and verve; Mark Steel essays some typically lusty drives as he contrasts the lot of the English crowd with that of its Caribbean counterpart; Kate Laven reveals how being the tournament's busiest reporter and not possessing an Adam's apple need not be mutually exclusive; Paul Weaver dissects England's sombre summer and recommends an extreme cure – amateurism; Graeme Wright casts an acute eye over the rebirth of his native New Zealand; Keith Booth reflects on the highs and woes of the official scorer, without whom ...

Elsewhere, Stephen Bates visits the swards of continental Europe; Andrew Shields offers that most elusive of journalistic creations: a balanced view of racism; Colin Shindler, doing his bit to commemorate the final season of the single-tiered county championship, stops hating Manchester United for five minutes and trains his loathing on Yorkshire. And last, but by no earthly means least, Simon Hattenstone, hotfoot from surviving an interview with Demis Roussos's kaftan, divulges his shameless passion for England's favourite pin-cushion, Graeme Ashley Hick. Enjoy.

Rob Steen, Alexandra Palace, November 1999

ACKNOWLEDGEMENTS

Merci biens to all the latest (plus a few of the usual) suspects: Kate, Tom, Kevin, Brian, Paul, Mark, Andrew, Simon, Keith, Stephen and Graeme for their sterling (all right, euro) contributions; Charles Frewin, Lance Bellers, Bobby and Carina Grossmark, the Two Toms (Petty and Waits), Sugar Ray, Robin Ventura, Kevin Spacey, Leslie and Alma Wolfson, Glen Watson, Hannah and Lionel Levy, Rita Kay, Jennifer Wingate, Anne, Jimmy, Peter and Ian Rothman, Aubrey and Miriam Gerber – for support and inspiration. And, above all, to the management: Anne, Laura, Josef, Evie and Woody.

Spinal Tap: cover quote – Courtney Walsh

Tom Jenkins is a Kentish Man
(he thinks). Taught wicket-
keeping at Sevenoaks School by
Paul Downton and practised
briefly at Sevenoaks Vine,
allegedly the world's oldest
cricket ground. Has worked for
the *Guardian*, *Sunday Telegraph*,
and *Independent*. British Young
Press Photographer of the Year
(1990), twice runner-up in British
Sports Photographer of the Year;
won Ilford Sports Photograph of
Year (1992 – Wasim Akram and
Chris Harris colliding) and Best
World Cup (soccer) Photograph
(1998). Sprayed incessantly by
Botham and water pistol during
1992 World Cup. Favourite
sporting experience: *that*
Australia-South Africa double-
header, 1999.

Wickedest wicket (joint)
Shoaib's yorker to Fleming in the
World Cup semi – unbelievable;
Tufnell dismissing McGrath to
win the sixth Test at The Oval '97
– the perfect end to a perfect day.

Soundest bite "Hey, Greigy!
The champagne's all right, but the
blackcurrant jam tastes of fish."
(Derek Randall in India)

Tom Jenkins
World Cup Gallery

SPUDS AND BUDS PAKISTAN V AUSTRALIA, HEADINGLEY

Brian Matthews
Flags and Banners

Brian Matthews

Brian Matthews was born
and brought up in St Kilda.
Appointed Lecturer in English at
Flinders University, South
Australia in 1969, he has been
visiting Professor at numerous
universities all over the world and
in 1997 became the Foundation
Director of The Europe-Australia
Institute at Victoria University,
Melbourne. Described as a writer
of "spare, polished stories" with a
"hilarious comic gift", he is well
known as an author, broadcaster
and columnist. *Louisa*, his biography of Henry Lawson's mother,
won the Australian Literary
Society's Gold Medal.

Wickedest wicket In 1993
I was working in London and
sneaked back to my flat for the
first day of the Ashes series: the
first ball I saw, Warne bowled
Gatting. It was so prodigious and
my timing seemed so incredibly
lucky I thought it was a doctored
replay – or something. No one
turns on the telly in time to see an
event like that!

Imperium: *command; absolute power; supreme or imperial power.*
Revolution: a complete overthrow of the established government.
Republic: a state in which the supreme power rests in the people and their elected representatives.

The Shorter Oxford English Dictionary

Prologue
AS I WRITE, AUSTRALIAN TROOPS are in East Timor at the head of a peacekeeping contingent attempting to bring calm to that terrorised country, while at home a furious row has erupted between the Prime Minister, Mr John Howard, and his predecessor, Mr Paul Keating, about the possibly domestic political motives – as Keating sees it – that may have dictated Howard's commitment of troops. Meanwhile, in Jakarta, the Indonesian government is accusing Australian soldiers of atrocities and orchestrated demonstrators are attacking Australian diplomatic premises and torching the flag.

Nationalist sentiment in Australia, normally mild-mannered and evoked by overseas sporting conquests or the sight of a Qantas Jumbo in a foreign port, has become temporarily more muscular and, like all nationalisms when displays of force and power are involved, slightly ugly. Across the South Pacific, nationalist fires, both metaphoric and actual, are flickering through a gloom of ignorance, misinformation and rumour. If Indonesia played cricket and was about to send a team to Australia for the antipodean summer, the date would probably be cancelled amid much acrimony. As it is, the actual fixture for this summer – a three-cornered competition between Australia, Pakistan and India – is teetering on the edge of destruction because of the war in Kashmir. What if India and Pakistan take on to the wide spaces of the MCG or the Gabba or the WACA ground in Perth the festering enmities which are yet again erupting at one of their perennial flashpoints? The kind of nationalism which dictators, military interlopers and war-hungry governments depend on is as harmful to cricket as it is to everything else.

And yet, and yet ... How often does cricket actually succumb to the worst kinds of nationalism, the kind that sets countries against each other, inflames border incidents, incites lies and invective? Without joining the cricket-is-a-training-for-life school, one can still say that the most nationalistic outbreaks in cricket are, by and large, forms of sledging. This is true even when, as in the present case of Pakistan and India, much more serious tensions exist and threaten. If sledging is the worst that happens, we should be thankful for cricket's apparent capacity to rise above the nastier nationalisms – and I don't say that only because Australians are the best sledgers.

(I) The Imperium

IT WAS MY TURN to be Australia and I'd won the toss and decided to bat. While I strapped on the single pad that constituted the entire stock of our available equipment (over and above an actual bat and ball), my mate – a chunky, 11-year-old, blond-headed scrapper whose name was Tod but whom we both saw as bearing an uncanny resemblance to Alec Bedser – warmed up at the other end. I would face "Bedser's" first ball in my guise as Arthur Morris and as soon as I picked up a sharp single or leg-glanced a three with the peculiar nonchalance that left-handers often bring to that shot, I would become Jim Burke.

Padded up and twirling my Gray Nicholls bat autographed by Neil Harvey and given to me that very Christmas by my parents, I gazed around the field – at the boxthorn bush at square leg, the stunted and decaying apple orchard at deep midwicket, the potato patch that would become my family's front lawn at point. Then I checked the exercise book lying open immediately behind the stumps, in which was recorded in a large, round, schoolboy hand my batting order. Morris, Burke, Hassett, Harvey, Miller … Quite a handy team. I carefully took block, settled into my stance and watched Tod Bedser come rolling in to bowl.

The first ball of the second Test for season 1949-50 pitched just short of a length and on middle stump, which it knocked out of the ground after not bouncing even an inch and skidding through like a lawn bowl. Sensation! Morris out first ball. Obviously, despite assiduous sweeping with my mother's best kitchen broom, some small pieces of gravel must have eluded our attention. The packed dirt track was a tough surface for bounce at the best of times; but sabotaged by gravel, it sapped the best deliveries of all resilience. As I recorded nought next to Morris' name and prepared to face up in the guise of Lindsay Hassett, I reflected that if my mother hadn't caught us using her broom and taken it away, the team might have got off to a much stronger start.

These England-Australia encounters went on interminably throughout the long summer. Their longevity was exaggerated by the fact that, unlike the real thing, our days were not necessarily consecutive. Play in a given Test might open on Thursday, continue Friday but then go into abeyance until the following Wednesday, when hostilities would be resumed. The reasons for these adjournments ranged from causes as satisfyingly realistic as a thunderstorm to decidedly embarrassing interventions like a peremptory recall home for one or other of us; or long detention-like chores such as digging the potato patch or cleaning out the chook pens; or actual house arrest for some misdemeanour or other; or a request to "do the messages". Because the latter meant a bicycle trip, it was an interruption doubly dreaded: it took up valuable time, as much as a couple of hours, but it also meant that the courier returned to the crease weary, hot, sweating and generally not focused.

Tod and I were convinced we'd invented this Test Match extravaganza (though reminiscence years later would reveal the fragility of that claim). None of our other friends indulged in it and

The New Ball

attempts to expand the personnel always ended in disputes and walk-
offs uncharacteristic of the game of cricket. So we spent hours and
hours together, bowling at each other, filling in the scores, enacting
dusty mimicries of first-class cricket's timeless and arcane rituals –
the toss, inspecting the strip of unmade track that was the "wicket",
announcing and setting a phantom field, sometimes even intoning
a commentary in a voice we imagined was a dead ringer for the rich,
basso profundo of Alan McGilvray – and then, for an hour or so after
"stumps", discussing the cut and thrust of the day's play and where
the advantage for the moment rested. I don't think either of us ever
cheated, despite the readily available opportunities to do so, and
when Tod's family, who were always a bit strange and vaguely
criminal, suddenly decamped to other, northern climes, a new
partner lasted only one Test with me because I caught him doctoring
his score during the tense second innings.

Aside from cricket, Tod and I shared a rabid interest in reading
Champion, *Rover* and the *William* books. We would discuss the
exploits of Rockfist Rogan and other luminaries of those "boys'
weeklies" and, when not engaged in our Test Match rivalry, we
would model our lives as nearly as possible on the ethos and activities
endlessly elaborated upon in the adventures of William and his
Outlaws and embroider this stereotype with evidence from the
school stories in *Champion* and *Rover*. We brewed, manfully drank,
but actually detested versions of both the licorice water and the
ginger beer to which William was so addicted. We ranged through
the nearby, dilapidated orchard with catapults constructed along
lines we understood to be the Outlaws' preferred model. We
inhabited a fragile cocoon of romance and fantasy which was always
on the verge of cracking apart if concentration flagged or disbelief
became suddenly unsuspended, and which was packed up and
temporarily forgotten when we returned to our families at the end
of each arduous day of Test cricket, hunting or roaming.

To gaze at the pitch for instance, in the intense heat of a January
afternoon, perhaps after the England openers had weathered Lindwall
and Miller's exhausting opening spell, and to see not the slightly
yellowing consistency of a three-day-old Test wicket but the ruts made
by Mr Davis's wood cart and the stones and rubble deployed by the

council in response to my father's vigorous complaints, and to admit that's what you were seeing, was death to the whole make-believe construction. And very bad for line and length.

BUT SOMETIMES REALITY was irresistible. On one of our hunting trips, during which we fired volleys of wildly inaccurate stones from our catapults at the local bird life with an apparently murderous abandon and in true and fond imitation of the Outlaws, I took aim at a Rosella – a bird of glorious, riotous colours not often seen down our way – and wiped it off its high, song-strung perch with an unprecedented and totally fluky direct hit. It was stone dead before it hit the ground and when I picked it up I saw that blood had spoiled the elegantly merging miracle of hues on its chest. I was shocked, appalled. Vaguely I recognised – though I wouldn't have put it in these terms – that this was not in the script. Somehow, we'd strayed off the stage and wandered outside into the harsh light, where there was no greensward, no neatly marked white creases; where our unvarnished and scarred stumps were stuck in the middle of a roadway and where birds died in agony if your aim was "lucky" enough.

That harshly lit world outside the theatre of our dreams was also populated with people who didn't understand our drama or wilfully refused to. Traffic was rare along the backtrack where our titanic struggles took place, but sometimes a car or a delivery van, their drivers almost invariably lost and looking like it, would trundle round the bend at the bowler's end (we didn't change ends – the pitch had only one usable section and, anyway, we had only three stumps) and bear down on us. We adopted the habit of getting out of the way and off the road with an ostentatious show of speed, goodwill and co-operation designed to compensate for the fact that we had left the stumps in the ground.

Every now and then, and to our utter stupefaction, a motorist would respond to this manoeuvre by running our stumps over. One driver actually broke two of them and signalled his satisfaction through the open window as he departed. Such occasions placed the whole fantasy under critical stress. Untutored though we both were in the ways of international cricket, having never seen a game and not being able to fall back on television to provide us with insights, we nevertheless were pretty certain that vehicular traffic was not one of the problems the teams encountered out in the middle – no matter where they were playing.

For just those three or four summers during which Tod and I advanced towards and attained our 12th year, doing so in a veritable welter of cricket and British boys' weeklies liberally embellished with William, I think we became rather imperial in our views and attitudes. Though to "be" Australia in our regular Ashes jousts was naturally the preferred and valued option, "being" England was an honourable – indeed, a more and more honourable – fate: if it hadn't become so, what would have been the point in persisting?

You had to feel all right about yourself as you ran into bowl in the guise of Brown or Bailey or Bedser; otherwise, you wouldn't bowl and bat well and you'd be thrashed. There were, after all, only two boys out on that track, not the two immaculately flannelled teams we saw in our imagination's gaze as we played. There were certain realities, certain facts that our cocoon of imagining, for all its elaborate fabric and strength, could never distort or blur. Neither of us, for example, was in the slightest doubt that when England, say, (represented by Tod) gave Australia the father of a hiding by an innings and 140 runs (all our scores, incidentally, ended in nought as each run counted for 10), it actually meant that Tod had made a terrible mess of me. Symbiosis between imagined team and the small boy carrying its entire burden of personality, performance and aspiration tightened ineluctably. So that, while an Australian bias in each of us was a given, we both with insidiously gradual effect came to respect, have exhaustive knowledge about, and even in certain ways admire – the Poms.

AIDED BY OUR diet of reading, an obsessive immersion in the game we thought we'd invented and a school curriculum that almost never recognised the existence of Australian writers, Australian history or the Australian vernacular, we very nearly attained in those three years of summers a condition above nationalism. We were cricketers; we represented "our country" – but our country was sometimes England. Though we, needless to say, didn't give the matter a thought, the entire structure and ambience of our Test Match series, with its transformation of national distinctions into the sporty "old enemy" formula and its code of manly conduct derived from the twin sources of cricket folk lore and boys' weeklies, was actually in close accord with the Anglophile attitude of Fifties Australia at large. And, though we didn't realise this either, the drama of our games was heavily underwritten by a sense of the then accepted, settled, Australia–Britain relationship.

Our dutiful attempts to stage "Tests" with South Africa, India and the West Indies – in line with what was happening in the real world – were at best perfunctory and, in one case if I remember rightly, suffered the unprecedented fate of being abandoned through waning interest. Looking back, I think this must have been because we found it difficult to achieve the necessary identification with either the teams, the individuals or – though again this would not have been our conscious thought – the cultures of those other cricket-playing nations. South Africa, India and the West Indies were just about as rare occurrences in the school curriculum as Australia itself. But England was everywhere: some of our politicians still referred to it as "home". Our Prime Minister, Sir Robert Menzies, declared himself "British to the bootstraps"; of the new queen, Elizabeth II, he proclaimed (to even her embarrassment): "I did but see her passing by/But I will love her till I die."

It's easy to overstate the impact of some of these influences and occasions in reminiscence, but I don't think there is much doubt about the fact that our attitude to cricket – the jewel in the crown of imperial games – was significantly shaped by the intensely Anglophile world in which we grew up and in which we actually played the game, even if only on a rough, outer suburban track. It was an attitude that comprised an over-developed reverence for the game's character-building capacities together with exaggerated respect for its English provenance. That there was no televised cricket (until 1956) against which we could measure our attitudes and intuitions was also immensely important. I remember seeing a brief newsreel snippet of Bradman's 1948 team practising shortly after their arrival in England. They were in the nets, but because I'd never seen players practising in six or seven nets at once, I became very

With republ
and insouc
was asserting
his team's
authority and
like an
in the

can confidence
ance, Waugh
his own and
dynamic
riding his luck
adventurer
New World.

confused – there seemed to be bowlers and batsmen everywhere – and somehow got the impression that this was how it must look in the middle, during a game! I wasn't prepared to show my ignorance and had to wait some months before I finally nutted it all out.

Curiously enough, during the time that these developments were taking place in our summer lives, our winters were probably intensifying the ambivalent, attenuated nature of our youthful nationalism. Because in winter we became totally absorbed with football, but it was the Australian invention, Australian Rules football. "Aussie rules" had no international competitive outlet or counterpart; as far as we were concerned, it was a Melbourne phenomenon: not only did it not focus you out to the world, on the contrary, it turned your gaze inwards, to one of Melbourne's inner suburbs – in my case, the gangster-ridden, smoky, cosmopolitan purlieus of St Kilda (a team for which, only a few years earlier, Keith Miller had played at full-back). Far from playing upon national feelings, football in Melbourne engendered the fiercest and most irrational parochialism. It was so divorced from national sentiment as to make that sentiment look redundant. On a cold, misty July Saturday in Melbourne, as the siren sounded and the ball was bounced to start yet another clash between the suburban titans, the long glaring days of summer and the idea of Australia being engaged in international contest seemed only a dream.

"Being" Australia; "being" England against Australia: taking block against that lone figure limbering up at the other end – the two of you carrying throughout the long, hot day the burden of the entire Antipodean or English strategy – that was our world of cricket. We were, of course, when it came to it, larrikin supporters of the Aussies, but our games, as much as the real stuff, were played in a lingering imperial rather than incipiently nationalist atmosphere. If the Empire was already burning, we didn't notice, but kept our Neronian heads down and played forward – the only way to survive on our pitch.

(II) The Revolution

BUT YOU COULDN'T MISS the flames when the revolution finally arrived. On his Test debut against England at Adelaide in 1971, Dennis Lillee grasped the opportunity with a ferocity that would become familiar. I saw every day of that match and I remember

Lillee, who was relatively unheralded, tearing in at breakneck speed, bowling very fast and conceding nothing to enervating heat or gusting wind. In the first innings he took five for 84. He would later reflect that, given his match payment of A$180, he had cost the Australian Cricket Board A$36 per wicket – a bargain whatever way you looked at it.

Lillee, in a more or less throwaway line to a journalist, was one of the first to make the radical proposal that players should be contracted to the Board and paid A$25,000 or A$30,000 per year. The Board's response to this idea, which in the early Seventies was attracting more and more attention among players and aspirant entrepreneurs, came initially in the form of a statement from the secretary, Alan Barnes. "The players are not professional," he said. "They are invited to play and if they don't like the conditions there are 500,000 other cricketers in Australia who would love to take their place." Just how readily Australia could replace almost an entire Test team with another as capable of coping with international competition would be trenchantly demonstrated when the "official" Australian team, shorn of World Series Cricket players, scraped in against India but was thrashed by the West Indies and England. Barnes' smug response was the reaction of the Imperium. He couldn't see the flames either.

After the 1975 tour of England, in which Australia retained the Ashes, players learned that while the Board had made a profit of A$78,000, their own share – A$182 per week for the duration of the 105-day tour – would not actually cover their costs. Against a background of growing discontent, the "Packer revolution" secretly got underway during 1976. Less than two months after the Centenary Test at the MCG in March 1977 news broke that Kerry Packer had signed up 35 of the world's elite cricketers to play a series of "Supertests" and one-day games during the 1977-78 Australian summer. By the time the rift was healed, Australia's cricketers were deservedly being treated and paid as professionals.

Recalling the stirring days of the "Packer revolution" 10 years after the event in a piece entitled "Glory, Then The Revolution", Tony Lewis asked what better time could there have been "to stir a revolution" than the aftermath of the Centenary Test: "The rulers were relaxed, partying and believing with every draught of armagnac that the good times were with them forever." Ian Wooldridge, who initially described the defectors as "the dogs of cricket", later adopted the same storm-the-barricades parlance in his account of the World Series Cricket court case: "Stubbornly the opposition refused to capitulate. It was convinced that God and the Establishment – most members of the British establishment acknowledge no difference between the two – must prevail." But, he continued, "World Series Cricket, or some such revolutionary institution, was always going to happen ... You cannot forever ... expect forelock-tugging subservience ..."

Lillee taunted: "Cricket was never going to be the same, who'd ever heard of cricketers wearing anything but white ... playing with a white ball ... playing at night? No wonder the Establishment purists damned near choked on their pink gins." Phil Wilkins saw the WSC players as heroes standing "in the firing line of the arch-conservative forces of moderation and Establishment stagnation". And David Hill, from Packer's Channel Nine, described "the howls of anguish" that he said greeted the broadcaster's new-look, technological cricket coverage: "... making a mockery of the game, etc., etc., ... retired colonels wrote huffing letters about never watching Channel Nine again ... retired cricketers demanded that such and such a commentator be replaced because, although he may have represented Australia in umpteen Tests, it was obvious to the writer who had played D Grade for the last 30 years that so-and-so knew nothing about the game."

These contributions and others like them were collected in a Channel Nine/Wide World of Sports publication called *Ten Turbulent Years* (1987) and they are remarkable for the repeated imagery of class war, outraged privilege and barricades terminology which, quite independently, most of the writers resorted to. (There is one other comparably consistent note throughout the book: the fat, purring undertone of self-satisfaction.) The picture they paint portrays anyone who is not actually ecstatic about "revolutionary", entrepreneurial cricket (which actually meant, above all, one-day internationals) and its media mentor, Channel Nine, as: elderly to old ("retired"); pompous, ridiculous ("colonel"); presuming superiority

("forelock-tugging subservience"); irrational and resistant to change
("huffing letters"); member of an elite, affluent group (drinking
armagnac and pink gin unlike the ordinary bloke with his Fosters
or XXXX); an unskilled, cricketing nonentity ("played D Grade for
the last 30 years").

More than 10 years further on, antagonisms have waned and the
straw men so ruthlessly demolished by the *Ten Turbulent Years*
writers have long since blown away. Old antipathies now seem
quaint and predictions made then (by me, among others!) that cricket
would be irreparably harmed have been happily proved wrong. It has
changed massively and changed in some ways that are regrettable,
but it still rolls on and Test cricket in Australia has recovered from
the poor relation status that Channel Nine attempted to impose on
it and has demanded equal and proper attention simply by virtue
of its continued success.

ONE-DAY INTERNATIONALS were marketed and touted with
furious intensity under the new regime. A new kind of audience was
wooed and won. A spurious nationalism that was simply
commercialism disguised was inculcated by means of endless
repetition: "C'mon Aussie, C'mon, C'mon" – a legacy from the
World Series days and the great split – was sung like an anthem, as
were certain advertising jingles, such as "I still call Australia home"
(eventually the accompaniment in the Qantas ad). Seasonal slogans,
emerging as early appetite-whetters ("Thunder Down Under"
among others), were also part of the package. No one could
remember or distinguish one one-day game from another once they'd
receded even a few weeks into the past.

This was no place for the kind of aficionado who could tell you that
Bradman gave two chances – on 264 and 345 – during his 452 not
out against Queensland in January 1930. No one could keep up with
the relentless rush of figures, graphs, run-rates, strike rates and other
ephemera spawned day after day, week after week by the "one-
dayers". Nobody wanted to. You just went along, watched the same
three teams playing each other time after time until they were a
(coloured) blur, enjoyed the often spectacular and exciting spectacle,
drank a little, some, or a lot of booze, and played your part in endless

circuits of the Mexican Wave if the action slackened even to the small extent of a scoreless over. If it were possible for something like the Bodyline incident to occur today in the one-day arena, the crowd wouldn't push down the fence – they very likely wouldn't notice straight away, being too intent on the Mexican Wave and the throwing in the air of 86,000 tonnes of litter which ritually accompanies it.

Translated on to television, the one-day games and, to a slightly lesser extent, Test cricket, became the vehicles for an advertising barrage of unprecedented concentration. When Australian cricket fans settle in front of their TV screens to watch Channel Nine cricket, they endure a couple of ads between every over, three or four when a wicket falls, a swathe of them during drinks and, quite often these days, a running advertisement for the car you can win in the current competition which actually resumes between each ball of an over with the commentating voice (somehow it always seems to be Tony Greig) doing the spruiking. The fragmentation is massive and any chance of enjoying one of cricket's great charms – its often leisurely unfolding, the mid-pitch conferences between overs, the captain earnestly conversing with his bowler, etc. – is lost. Not to mention the difficulty under these conditions of getting a sense of the process of the game, its subtle ebbs and flows as distinct from its great shifts of pace and fortune.

It must be added, though, that Australian watchers of cricket on TV have scarcely raised a whimper in protest at all this, which has been going on now with increasing intensity for 20-odd years. So that descriptions of it such as this one always feel uncomfortably like a whinge and can easily be made to look petty by the massive disdain of the corporate giant. The interesting thing is that opposition to Channel Nine's version of cricket is also often treated as if it's a kind of betrayal, un-Australian ...

So, what price revolution? Apart from its crucial success in securing proper reward for the professionalism of the players – and they are now properly rewarded – like many revolutions, this one has ended up skin-deep. Coloured clothes, doctored rules, third umpires, stumpcams and various other applications of technology, are neither here nor there; some are good, some not so good. The game of cricket seems to endure it all more or less imperturbably. WG Grace would recognise it instantly and Bradman enjoys and approves of much of what has evolved. There is no substantial aspect of the actual game of cricket at the end of the millennium that you could point to and say: that is the result of the Revolution. The most enduring images and reminders are the Mexican Wave, the close identification of advertisers and their products with cricket, and the silencing more or less of the "cricket buff" – the fan who eats, sleeps and breathes the game, who is suffused not so much with a nationalistic fervour as with a reverence for the game itself. Such characters have not disappeared but they are no longer influential and their obsession is seen as quaint and fusty.

(III) The Republic

IN THE DAYS of the Imperium – when, so it seemed, we were British to the bootstraps – Steve Waugh would have maintained a dignified silence as he watched Herschelle Gibbs drop the sitter that turned the game. Reliable reports assure us that he was not silent and that what he actually said was: "What's it feel like to drop the World Cup?" If Alan Barnes' lofty dismissal of the cricketers' claims to professionalism was a remark of the Imperium, this now famous exchange was in the spirit of the Republic. This is not mainly because it's a larrikin jibe (which it is), but because its provenance is the free spirit, the quintessentially Australian ironic temperament that "doffs its lid to no man", will always "have a go", and is turning away from archaisms like royalty, inherited privilege and some of the outmoded attitudes and behaviour that a few hard-line traditionalists insist is part of the game's moral fibre.

The idea of Australian cricket's proud and victorious profile being claimed for republican or monarchist laurels is actually not at all fanciful. As discussion about the possible Australian republic began to gather some momentum towards the end of 1999, somebody in the monarchist camp came up with the claim that Mark Taylor, Australia's recently retired and all-conquering Test captain, had declared for the monarchy and against a republic. In the ensuing sensation, Taylor was at pains to deny this attribution, insisting that he had not come to any firm position so far. And the Prime Minister, Mr Howard (a declared monarchist), was forced to distance himself from the controversy by denying any discussions with or overtures to Taylor on the question of Australia's future head of state. Underlining his non-involvement, Howard said that if he'd had the good fortune to talk at length to Taylor, he would not have wasted the opportunity by talking about Republicanism; he would have got down to serious topics such as cricket.

In making this comment, Howard – apart from attracting criticism from people who objected to what they saw as an unacceptably frivolous response – was conforming to a model that is obviously deeply etched into his imagination. It derives partly from a perception of his political hero, Sir Robert Menzies, who was genuinely knowledgeable about cricket and famous for contriving to see days and days of England–Australia games in both hemispheres despite the cares and commitments of office; and partly from the broader stereotype of blokes in Australia being cricket-mad, steeped in its lore and preferring it to real life whenever possible – a stereotype long ago overrun by the pace and intricacy of events.

Taylor himself remarked of this apparent obsession that Howard was "a cricket tragic" – someone more thoroughly enslaved to the game and all its lore and ramifications than even the players themselves. But such enslavement was much easier when cricketers were part of a grand design and knew their place in it; and the "tragic" knew his (or her) place as well. It is outdated in the age of affluent professionalism, superstars of bat and ball, outrageous individualism and cricket crowds notable not for intent concentration, respectful silences and attention to scorecards, but for vast and constantly altering diversity and casual serendipity of attitude, loyalty and opinion.

In the last two decades of the 19th century, while politicians from the five mainland colonies and Tasmania were struggling to hit upon ways of unifying their disparate territories under a federal banner, a cricket team made up of representatives from those same colonies and calling itself "Australia" was performing various mighty deeds in both hemispheres. There was for a start the "Ashes" Test at The Oval where Fred "The Demon" Spofforth told his teammates, "This thing can be done", and then, with the aid of Harry Boyle, went and famously did it. And then there was the triumph of 1897-98, a 4–1 victory over England by "Australia" even as the delegates to the Australasian Convention were beginning meetings in Adelaide to make yet another attempt at tying the federal knot. The international cricket team was known and greeted as "Australia" and the "Australians" long before 1901 when Australia was born officially and constitutionally.

Though the present team is known and greeted in many ways and by varied nomenclature, not all of it admiring, it is not fanciful to see them anticipating events as their illustrious cricketing forebears did on the eve of federation, to see them as already a republican team in the looming shadow of the November referendum. Such a view has of course nothing to do with individual team members' preferences and views: it's an impression gained from the ambience of the team and from its style. Using republic as it is used in the expression "the Republic of Letters", we see the Australians as independent, self-confident, bonded with a freewheeling egalitarianism, prodigiously talented and ready to take on the world with these talents. This is not a group that reminds us of monarchies or dictatorships; these are not "subjects" but free men.

Under the present constitutional arrangements, Australians are the subjects of the Queen of England. When Steve Waugh turned his saturnine, baggy green-capped visage towards the aghast Gibbs, he was nobody's subject. With republican confidence and insouciance, he was asserting his own and his team's dynamic authority and riding his luck like an adventurer in the New World. Admittedly, if you're going to turn your republican face defiantly towards opposition and the cautionary winds of constraint, it helps if you win now and then. If you go on to win the World Cup, well, people write articles about you ... ⟫

ASIA'S GAUCHOS (I) BANGLADESH V NEW ZEALAND, CHELMSFORD

ASIA'S GAUCHOS (II) INDIA v ENGLAND, EDGBASTON

Kevin Mitchell

Oh, What A Lovely War

Kevin Mitchell, born in Malawi in 1950, raised in Roscommon, Birmingham and Kurri Kurri, NSW, finished off in north London over past 25 years – is chief sports writer at *The Observer*. Still bowling slow left-arm after 38 seasons, he has taken more wickets than he has scored runs. Finally hit a six last year, a thick outside edge over third man on a tiny ground in Surrey. Campaigns for abolition of all lbw restrictions. If it hits, it's out!

Wickedest wicket Richie Benaud, smoothest action of them all, bowling Peter May around his legs at Old Trafford in 1961. Coming around the wicket, he made PBH sweep, a shot he didn't favour. Pitched in the rough way outside leg, hit off. Super delivery.

Soundest bite "Bournemouth, Get A Life" – banner hanging from a stand at heaving, drunken Bridgetown when England beat West Indies in 1994 to break a non-winning sequence of 59 years.

Many years ago, I worked for a while in Sydney with an entertaining collection of rascals who passed their daylight hours as sports journalists on *The Sun* – the city's afternoon tabloid that was not owned by Rupert Murdoch – and, by night, harboured the illusion they were the combined reincarnation of Wyatt Earp and Errol Flynn.

"Keep your money in your pocket, son," was the kindly advice I got when I arrived. The speaker was a lovely man called Johnny Dwyer, a Queenslander who'd played hockey for Australia in the 1956 Olympics and cricket with Don Tallon. Like "Deafy", I didn't listen. Due largely to the publishing acumen of a comedian called "Young Warwick" Fairfax, *The Sun* has since folded. But I'm thankful. Sort of. That office, fenced off from the rest of the newspaper like a Borstal rec yard, introduced me to a gambling culture you would not find anywhere else. All week we'd bet: on the trots, dogs, horses, cricket, football, fights, on which car the parking cop would nick in the street below our fourth-floor office.

Friday, though, was the big day. Led by the turf editor Bill Casey and his chief racing writer Max Presnell we lunched at the Old Tai Yuen, a restaurant in Chinatown run by the ever-smiling Stanley Wong, who bought most any horse Max told him to and never complained if the nag didn't win.

Over Stanley's best chicken and black bean sauce – served up with comic obsequiousness by Henry the Waiter, the bottom of whose trousers consistently failed to reach the top of his socks – we'd discuss various betting coups and disasters, none more enthusiastically among us than the deputy sports editor, Kenny "Hang Dog" Laws. Hang Dog (so called because he laughed constantly) would eventually wind up his legendary punting endeavours, about the time a bus ran over his leg outside the office pub years later, possibly after drink had been taken. Last I heard, he'd join the Hare Krishnas.

As an hors d'oeuvre to a session at Stanley's, we would settle down in the office after Friday's first edition, about 9am, for a few hands of euchre, four-handed (euchre is a whist variant, popular in Australia and, I understand, around Bristol). They were all keen players: Hang Dog, Spock, Ernie, Little Ernie (his son), Zorba, Porky, Seldom Seen, Glargy – who was once buried up to his neck at low tide on a Sydney beach by gentlemen demanding payment of a gambling debt – and King, who used to raffle his wages on occasional desperate Thursdays. To borrow from the late Richard Baerlien, they all "bet like men". If you lost, you could be reduced to triple-decker prawns and a cup of Chinese tea by the time you reached Stanley's.

When I very occasionally got into a game, I was lumbered with John Benaud (he would contend he was lumbered with me), the sports editor and, for a while in the Seventies, one of the most exciting batsmen in the world. He was as crap at euchre as I was, although I never heard him admit it. That morning, however, Benners and I were famously in a position to beat the best players in the office, Zorba and Porky, coming from 10–nil down to 10–all, first to 11. The office held its breath.

Zorba dealt, turned up a heart, an eight as I remember. My call. I could hardly keep a straight face when I looked at my hand: the five biggest hearts in the pack. A gift. Ignoring all card etiquette, I went for a grandstand finish – four points, even though we only needed one. Telling a disbelieving Benaud to take a rest, I "went alone" against the other two and, in so doing, had to order Zorba to pick up the eight, which made hearts trumps. Then, without going through the formalities, I laid down my right and left bower (the jack of hearts and its off-suit), ace, king and queen with a riverboat flourish. Unbeatable! Zorba refused to pay. He said the rules stipulate I should have played the hand out, card by card. No arguing. "Bet with your head, Little Jesus [don't ask]," he said, pocketing the stake. "Never bet with your heart. Mug's game." Zorba was a man who knew something about life's tricky bits.

Benaud swore. The rest cracked up. I'd blown $200 a corner, not to mention destroying a few sidebets. I didn't go to Stanley's that Friday. Aussies are like that, which is the point of this story. Like humour, gambling is no laughing matter. And so, 20 years later, to Lord's on Sunday, June 20, 1999, and the final of the World Cup. Very serious business indeed.

AT THE START of the tournament, there were only three teams I had considered backing: Australia, Pakistan and England, and now two of them had made it all the way. I looked at Shane Warne as he warmed up in the nets, and Rick "Punter" Ponting. Mark Waugh, too. These guys, gamblers from the Hang Dog school, would back themselves here (metaphorically, of course) to beat Pakistan. You could smell it. Like Zorba, they knew all about life's tricky bits. And they knew all about Pakistan. They'd accused some of them of trying to rig a Test match, for crying out loud.

The Aussies were on a roll of six wins after a rotten start to an enthralling tournament. They had just seen off South Africa in the most remarkable one-day game of them all, when, to almost universal mirth, Klusener had run himself out going for a run that wasn't there, a euchre four-pointer instead of one. In the match before, which South Africa should have won, Steve Waugh, en route to the century that secured victory, was afforded the golden moment of rebuke when dropped by Herschelle Gibbs, prematurely celebrating a gimme catch. 'What's it feel like to drop the World Cup, Herschelle?'

These Aussies were the spiritual heirs of Lillee and Marsh, those pragmatists who'd taken the 500–1 about England pulling off a miracle against them at Headingley in 1981, and collected – despite their own best efforts, it must be said. They would not be swayed by sentiment, and you could be sure they reckoned they had the measure of Pakistan. It was, as they say in 500, a lay-down misere.

You sensed they knew something we did not. So, why was my money on Pakistan? Because, six weeks before, it had not seemed so straightforward.

IT HAS ALWAYS struck me as an endearing touch, the way that people on the subcontinent refer to their grown-up Test cricketers as "the boys". It rings of avuncular regard, as well as a hankering after innocence, maybe. Sunny, happy days ... Who was I to say it wasn't so? With an eye on a possible investment, I wanted nothing more than to believe Wasim Akram that rainy afternoon in Hampstead, a week before the tournament. The day he swore "the boys" would do their best to win the World Cup.

I had arrived at Pakistani House in north London way too early. A typically grand Hampstead brick pile, with big gates and sweeping driveway, just right for long, dark-windowed limos. Smiling consulate heavies, bearing umbrellas in the early-summer downpour, inspected my invitation and led me down the side of the house into the reception marquee at the back, where the High Commissioner, Mr Mian Riaz Samee, was waiting with the eagerness of a dentist looking for loose teeth. His Excellency dripped cordiality as steadily as the rain that splashed on his splendid rosebushes outside.

"The boys" were coming down from their hotel in Derby, he said, and might have been held up on the wet roads. Terrible, terrible weather. Really hot back in Pakistan now. Always hot. You have never been? You must come and see it for yourself ... Yes, "the boys" could put "recent controversies" behind them, he said, and win the World Cup. They're 12-1, you say ...?

Time to move on to the sandwiches, I reckoned, mingle a bit with the gathering throng. Richard Pybus had been brought in at the last minute as Pakistan's coach. In the green team blazer, and looking the part in an athletic, short-back-and-sides sort of way as he hovered near the biscuits and tea, the former Minor Counties fast bowler from Carlisle explained he had been asked to help out by the team's assistant manager, who had been at university with him. That did not seem so mysterious. Jobs are regularly handed out in cricket like that. But, in the absence of alcohol, the recognised social lubricant in these situations, we skated over the circumstances that had facilitated his appointment.

Pybus was having his few weeks in the sun only because – depending on which version you accepted – Javed Miandad had either walked out on or been relieved of, the coaching job, after accusing the players of not trying when losing to England at the warm-up tournament in Sharjah. Or throwing it, to you and me. It was a nothing match, and nearly all the allegedly dodgy ones were nothing matches, they said. Who could be sure? Pybus, who had been with the team for a fortnight, would only say: "The boys are very, very confident. They are a very together team. 12–1? Not bad."

I would hear different versions of Pakistan's togetherness before the tournament was over, but there seemed no reason to doubt that this was Pybus's considered impression. A pleasant man who talks good cricket – and who would quietly hand over the coaching to the colourful Mushtaq Mohammed by the time the World Cup got serious then subsequently succeed Mushtaq's successor, Wasim Raja – he might have been a professional himself had he not given up his early playing years to study. Shortish for a fast bowler, and stocky, he had been a bit rapid, he said, but, if you haven't been noticed by the time you're 21 or so, you're struggling. You do not get noticed much at Suffolk. He saw a better future in coaching, and went to South Africa. From the understanding way he talked about township cricket, Pybus did not seem to be one of those apartheid-era, eyes-shut mercenaries. And he cared about his Pakistan charges. "The boys". I wanted to know more about the character of these guys.

Saqlain Mushtaq was 22 with a shaky hold on English, but who needs to talk like Melvyn Bragg when you can make a cricket ball talk? He might be the best off-spinner of them all one day. Here he was anonymity itself as he sipped at his water. "They should wear name tags," a guest said, passing Saqlain by; the legendary subcontinental love for cricket did not, apparently, reach all corners of London's Pakistan community.

"He's a terrific young bloke," Pybus said of Saqlain, "like all of them. Says very little, because of the language, but he's not one to boast about his bowling. Very unassuming. Nicest bloke in the team." He seemed tough enough to me, this kid who had learnt his cricket in the dustier parts of Islamabad. For three years Saqlain had plied his weird off-spinners and unpickable, dipping, curling leg-breaks; more often than not, he'd been Pakistan's matchwinner at the end of tight one-day games. He would not crack. A banker.

Whatever Pybus said, young Saqlain was in worldly company. Once Pakistan's Test team was packed with moneyed, Oxbridge types who played uncorrupted by worldly concerns; now the side was earthier, bristling with ambitious cricketing hustlers not afraid of an argument with the opposition – although as obsequious as Henry the Waiter with their paymasters, whoever those might be.

A friendly Pakistani businessman who gave me a lift to the tube station later, said there were some people at the reception who knew nothing about the game, who were there only to be seen. They were the ones, rich, long-term expats more familiar with the regal Mohammeds and Khans of the past, who knew little about the new street boys, and did not trust them. But there were others, in the bookmakers shops of Bombay, in Dubai and Lahore and Karachi and Sharjah, who knew many of these players very well. Who knew them best, I wondered?

As that wet Friday spun out in a convivial, alcohol-free hum, there was a dissonant contribution from Shoaib Akhtar, whose season in Northern Ireland had injected his musical Rawalpindi accent with a Gaelic burr, and the odd colloquialism. ("Knackered I am," he would say after a hard day's work against South Africa.) However it came out, you believed him when he talked about his commitment. Like Darren Gough, Shoaib had only one gear: overdrive.

The Rawalpindi Express looked quick standing still, as they used to say of Nijinsky (the horse, not the dancer). His thick, black hair flopped over deep brown eyes that could switch from sleepy to electrified on that rush to the crease, and, in the gloom of the tent, his pearl-white smile leavened the stiff protocol. You could see that Shoaib was the beating heart of the team, maybe even more so than his captain. He, too, promised he would "do my best". It was something of a team mantra – or maybe insurance.

We'd not met before but Wasim smiled with the over-eager warmth of a man who needed friends. Back in Lahore, they were screaming for his blood or his coronation, depending on results.

After all this was over, they beat up his brother, a bookmaker. And they would howl indignantly when the losing finalists returned without their captain, who stayed behind to play for Smethwick in Birmingham and then extended his stay, behind a microphone for Channel 4, a strangely nervous contributor of opinions on the series between England and New Zealand.

And months after that, Chris Lewis would tell the *News Of The World* that a stranger from India had offered him £300,000 to introduce him to Alan Mullally and Alec Stewart with a view to their affecting the result of the Old Trafford Test (in which Mullally did not play). Odd. The paper identified the stranger as a "sports promoter" called Ashim Kheterpal. Wasim's mother would ask Pakistan to give her son peace and space.

As ever, there had been no shortage of rumours, even before the tournament. Sceptics outnumber romantics in my game by about 100 to 1 – which were the sort of odds you might have got that afternoon on Bangladesh beating Pakistan by 62 runs a month later in Northampton; two months before, Pakistan had crushed them by 152 runs, with 10 overs to spare, in a triangular tournament in Dhaka. But what did I know?

Anyway, here we were, in a tent in Hampstead, drinking tea and being polite. Wasim said "the boys" were fine, and, of course, they would do "their very best". I couldn't think of a thing to say. His Excellency moved through the deferential gathering like a bright fluffy cloud, all silver lining. Wasim took up the chat slack. "You have no idea the pressure on the boys! There are things written back in Pakistan, India too, in newspapers and magazines, by people I have never met, writing all sorts of things I've never said. You know the sort of things. It is useless. We must not let such stuff affect us."

Wasim was sweating. I'd heard he was diabetic and had to inject himself with insulin four times a day. He got tired. Of his wavering sugar levels, and of all the questions, no doubt. You had to feel for him, a hero with a physical and spiritual burden that would break ordinary men. A prisoner of circumstance, with no exit, no options. He was a cricketer. He was the captain. He was toast.

On cue, an excited woman worked her way through the small crowd that had formed around Wasim and begged him to do as he was promising. Fairly *begged* him. "All my Indian friends," she said, "you must win it so I can say to them that Pakistan are the best team in the world, the champions. You simply *must*. You have to prove to everyone that these stories about gambling on matches are not true." I have not seen a cornered tiger, but Wasim looked every inch the human equivalent, just as, at the urging of Imran Khan, he and his team-mates had done in Melbourne one grand night in 1992, the night they mauled England to win the World Cup.

Wasim nodded to the woman and her friends, his smile weak, his eyes sadder than a dying tiger's. She slipped away, content in the reflection of his celebrity, maybe because he looked so utterly vulnerable. Within five weeks or so, he would experience, not for the first time, the awful descent from talisman to object of scorn.

BACK TO HARD-HEADEDNESS. Nothing like a bit of inside information before putting your money down. So, having tried to gauge the mood of the players at Pakistani House, I rang Sarfraz Nawaz before it all kicked off for the lowdown on Pakistan, whom I figured might be good value at 12–1. If the lowdown is what you're looking for, it doesn't get lower or more down than the view "Saff" can give you. After years of tipping the bucket on former teammates he reckoned were cheats, he had gained a reputation as not so much a loose cannon as a howitzer rolling down the north face of the Eiger without brakes. This was not fair, according to Ron Body, a London-based New Zealand acquaintance who knows something of the internal workings of Pakistani cricket. "You could not get a more open character than Saff," Ron said. "It's just that sometimes he is too honest for his own good."

Saff spoke at that time from a position of strength. He was Pakistan's fast-bowling coach, having been appointed after a stint as a minister in charge of sport, and had the ear of the ruling regime. He held clinics in Lahore and Karachi, uncovering new talent, and had worked on the actions of most of the leading fast bowlers, including Waqar Younis, who would play little part in the World Cup less because of a knee injury than his lingering feud with Wasim, and with Shoaib. "Some people have tried to get him to cut down his run-up," he said. "But I told him that would be wrong, not natural

Wasim was a **prisoner** of circumstance. He was a cricketer. He was the **captain.** He was toast for him." So he had preserved for our delectation one of the most thrilling sights in modern cricket, that wild-eyed sprint that invariably delivered the excitement it promised. Would he deliver on 20 June? Sarfraz was of the opinion that, if Pakistan's batsmen got the runs, the bowlers would always win it for them. Meanwhile, he had battles of his own. When the day of the final came, the move by his enemies back home to get rid of Sarfraz was already in motion.

ABOUT A YEAR earlier, the Indian newsagent near my house and the Pakistani brothers a few doors away in the corner shop had sent off for their package of tickets. They all know and love their cricket. We swapped intelligence and convivial bullshit most days, in between the purchase of fish fingers, bus passes and the like, and discussed Shoaib and Dravid and Atherton and Warne. For the World Cup they would take up their positions on nationalist lines, with only symbolic mutual hostility – even as their countrymen were killing each other in Kashmir – and always with some residual sympathy for England, their home. I fantasised about Norman Tebbit bumping into his bête noir, the cricket-mad American iconoclast Mike Marqusee, in that selfsame corner shop.

They had not received all the tickets they were promised. None of us was stunned by this news, just let down. They suspected they were not being treated seriously, that the big games of the World Cup had been hived off for MCC members, for the touts, for corporate entertainers, for anybody but the guys down the corner shops. But they swapped tickets here and there from the allocation that did come their way and they just about got their quota of not-bad matches during the early rounds. They headed off to Hove (where India fell in a heap) and Northampton and Taunton. Getting to see the final at Lord's was going to be another game of soldiers altogether. Not to mention the nights leading up to the big day, and what a guy called Jim told them about Ijaz Ahmed.

Way before all that, to Cardiff to see my possible investment, the Aussies, playing New Zealand. Australia looked scratchy beating the out-of-sorts West Indies and complacent in beating Scotland, but maybe that was a sign of cool confidence. At Sophia Gardens they were mullahed by Roger Twose and Chris Cairns. Over drinks in the club bar with Bruce Wilson, an Australian correspondent living in London whose cv is as good as Hemingway's (Vietnam, Washington, Twickenham, Kosovo, Wimbledon, Lord's – you name it), and my similarly well-travelled *Observer* colleague, Eddie Butler, the consensus was that Australia might be strong enough over the long haul to win it. Best not be carried away with Bruce's partisan enthusiasm, though. Bet with your head, son. Wait and see.

AND WHAT OF the hosts, the team my heart wanted to win? After we'd emigrated to Australia in the Fifties – assisted passage, a six-year-old 10-quid kid on a grand adventure – I would sit up with my dad in bed and listen to John Arlott on the radio, unsure if the undulating voice that crackled through the glowing brown bakelite box was the accurate verbal representation of his beloved Hampshire or the thousands of miles of ocean it had to cross in relaying the cricket from "home". It was Arlott on Trueman, on May, on Barrington, on anything he cared to talk about. That's what sealed it. How could I ever switch allegiance? The heart ruled again.

If ever a cricket team – a team of sportsmen representing their country at any discipline, for that matter – were designed to confound supporters with their predictable inconsistency, England were that team. I did not go along with the view that they were in essence a poor collection of cricketers, even after they had limped out of the tournament against India. To me, they simply lacked purpose, cohesion and hardness, the smarts of Zorba and the steel of Steve Waugh. And my financial backing.

WHAT NORMALLY HAPPENS at these international sporting events – from the Olympics to France '98, and the world underwater hockey championships, for all I know – is that the journalists, who get in free, are really nice to the organisers (some of whom can be irritating jobsworths, but most of whom are eager young volunteers) while they are picking up their complimentary bags and other trinkets and then spend a month complaining about the phones, the free sandwiches, travel arrangements, lack of access and information, accommodation... Well, it has to be said: the sandwiches were appalling.

The New Ball

I was thinking of mentioning this to the lads in the corner shop (whose sandwiches are no great shakes). Most of the mainstream correspondents and columnists were more earnest about their complaints, and the man taking the flak was Lord MacLaurin, the chairman of the England and Wales Cricket Board, a chap. MacLaurin, unfortunately, also has something of the Duke of Edinburgh about him, a talent for the gaffe. And we in the comment business are not known for letting gaffes go harmlessly by, however nice the free bag is. This would be "a carnival of cricket", he'd said. We knew it was wishful thinking on a comic scale. Sophia Gardens, Hove, Taunton, Bristol, and Castle Avenue, Dublin? Come on.

In his zeal to take cricket to new markets, Lord Tesco had cocked it up. The World Cup got off to a crowded, disjointed start in inappropriate venues, with real fans unable even to get in, especially at Hove, where hundreds of Indian supporters watched the game against South Africa from the balconies of flats overlooking the time-locked county ground. And MacLaurin then chose the height of his "carnival of cricket" to proclaim that the number of foreign players in English cricket was a reason everyone else was better than England. He really did say "They come over here ..." Maybe he was capable of more irony than I gave him credit for.

This Little Englander nonsense will surely fade one day. The evidence was there for everyone to see, finally, that the future of the game is multi-coloured. Look at the makeup of the England lineup. Look at the faces in the crowd, from Edgbaston to Old Trafford. Listen to the kids in the street. Lord's does not own cricket. It did not own the final either.

Come the day, a wet, cathedral-grey Sunday morning, Wasim woke at the Royal Garden Hotel in west London, put together his insulin to go with his morning meal, and checked his cricket gear, like he had a thousand times. In the same hotel, Steve Waugh went through the same ritual. Minus the insulin. But with as much adrenalin.

The generals were ready. So were their foot soldiers. The short journey across London to St John's Wood would be tense for everyone, but not unfamiliar. Most of them had fought many times before.

The South Africans, still recovering from the devastation of losing in the final over of their semi-final against Australia, were also on the move. Home. Someone passed Lance Klusener in the marbled foyer and offered his condolences. "Zulu", never one for chat, walked quietly by. At Lord's, security guards were ejecting a Pakistani fan who'd slept at the ground overnight. In north London, as Stoke Newington Church Street woke up in its slow, suburban way, I stopped in at the corner shop to apologise to the guys for not getting them a ticket for the final. One of the brothers got in anyway, through a friend, and the others would watch it on TV, as they always suspected they would, while looking after the shop. Life goes on.

A few miles away, traffic growled around the streets of the world's most famous cricket ground. Green flags draped green-shirted shoulders, the owners of which shouted hysterically in the rain. Touts busied themselves on the wet pavement among the supporters, few of whom seemed to be Australian. A slow summer for back-packers, barmaids and dentists in London, maybe.

And we would discover inside what we had feared all along: Lord's was packed with members. "What that Michael Parkinson doesn't realise," said one bacon-and-egger from under his straw hat, sniping at the establishment bogeyman who writes in the establishment paper, the *Daily Telegraph*, "is that we own every bloody brick in this place. We should not have to pay to get in." But today they did. A few thousand of them had boycotted the opening matches here, protesting in their typically high-handed way. Not now. This was a day out, old boy.

Several thousand Pakistanis hung from the scaffolding on a building under construction across the road. The police left them there for an hour or so before moving in, also dispersing fans who had somehow got on to the roof of the nearby hotel; most went home to their TVs, but many stayed, wandering up and down outside the ground, looking through the gates, asking the score. From inside, witnessing the Pakistan collapse, you wondered why they bothered – although, really, you knew. They cared.

I bumped into Marqusee – wearing his Bangladeshi colours. We exchanged rants about the old guard and then, beer in hand, got back to the business of witnessing what would turn out to be a uniquely unsatisfying yet intriguing end to a marvellous five weeks of cricket. There are resignations to reality and there are abject capitulations.

What Pakistan showed the world that Sunday was most definitely the latter. How could "the boys" let everyone down like this? Had they no respect for my investment?

I always thought the Bangladesh result was suspect but I don't think Pakistan threw the final (you have to pinch yourself writing this). In conversation with the Pakistan cricket writer Qamar Ahmed beforehand, it was obvious that this tournament was the last throw of the dice for many of them, as sitting in a drawer back in the Lahore office of Justice Malik Qayyum, the judge appointed to investigate alleged match-rigging from earlier allegations, was the completed report. "If they win," said Qamar, "the report stays in the drawer."

I didn't wholly buy the logic. At the time of writing, after many of his deadlines had passed, Qayyum's report was still in the drawer. At a press conference in London in September, nevertheless, the new Pakistan board reinstated Wasim as captain having suspended him pending Qayyum's verdict. By the time you read this, a scapegoat or two might have been produced, but the status quo will remain largely undisturbed. Whatever, the stakes were huge. It was not in the players' interest to lose, whatever the outside interferences of bookmakers from Bombay. I am reasonably convinced that what happened in that final is that Pakistan were overcome by their own anxiety, their desperation to win – not to mention the foolishness of one or two of their players, which is a more culpable flaw.

A couple of weeks later, acting on a tip from one of the boys in the corner shop, we investigated what had been going on in the Pakistan camp in the days leading up to the final. What we were told was so at odds with the feeling of commitment I had detected in Hampstead five weeks earlier, and in contradiction of the whitewash that followed, I found it hard to believe.

A driver called Jim, assigned to chauffeur the team, said he had taken Ijaz Ahmed and a few other members of the team to a casino near Baker Street on the Friday night before the final. This was hardly ideal preparation for what Wasim had described only hours earlier as "the biggest game of my life". And, without wishing to sound like a hypocritical Catholic, gambling and drinking do not sit easily with the disciplines of Islam, surely.

Ijaz, it was alleged, stayed at the casino until near dawn, before being ejected after a scuffle with a member of staff. We were told that the captain had also been out in the West End, along with Saqlain. Even Shoaib had been slipping past the team guards during the tournament to enjoy himself. All charges were denied. But we also learned that the Pakistani secret service had been monitoring the team's behaviour throughout the tournament and had evidence of curfews being consistently broken. There was more to this than the results of mere cricket matches. Later, Wasim would admit to "some wrongdoing" during those five weeks. No specifics.

Were the stories true? Part of me said "so what?" After all, I worked in a culture that lauded such behaviour. I was a graduate of Stanley's and the euchre school. Looking around the press box, the betting throughout the World Cup was never less than steady. Jack Bannister, bless him, is a bookmaker. On England's last tour of West Indies, several of the correspondents made a killing on the unexectedly good showing of Angus Fraser through spread betting. I know county players who regularly bet on themselves, even though ECB regulations forbid it. Paul Smith, drummed out of the game after tabloid salivations about his interesting private life, told me when we met at Edgbaston for the England-India game that cricket is far from the all-white innocent pastime the public imagine. He'd say no more, though.

But this was the big one. This was the World Cup Final. Whatever your thirst for the good life or a scam, you put those considerations aside when it matters; it's small enough a sacrifice for the trust people have put in you to represent them at the game's highest level. You are playing for them even more than for yourself.

At the *Observer*, we were very confident of our sources but, as ever in Pakistan cricket, it was impossible to be completely sure, to divine truth from rumour. There are so many factions in the game there, not to mention in politics and society in general, you will never get an opinion from within that is not coloured by affiliation to one cabal or another. Sarfraz believed the stories. Wasim, naturally, did not. Back in Pakistan they rioted. As Wasim said they would.

A mug's game? ◑

LANCE A LOT KLUSENER DRIVES DURING ONE OF HIS HABITUAL
MATCHWINNING ONSLAUGHTS, THIS TIME V SRI LANKA

ZULU IN DISGUISE WITH GLASSES KLUSENER BEFORE NERVES OVERCAME VERVE

Kate Laven
Music To Watch Boys By

Kate Laven BA (Hons),
worked in advertising before
heading to Australia selling cars
and teaching on a cattle station.
Returned to Portsmouth in 1990
to retrain as a journalist and
spent the next seven years at
the *Southern Daily Echo* in
Southampton, reporting on
business, motoring and cricket.
In 1997, turned freelance and
now specialises in cricket and
yachting.

Wickedest wicket
Ian Botham's dismissal of Jeff
Thomson in Australia's second
innings, Fourth Test, Melbourne,
December 1982, giving England
victory by three runs (Tavaré
and Miller juggled the ball in the
slips before Miller finally took
the catch).

Soundest bite "What's it feel
like to drop the World Cup,
Herschelle?" (Steve Waugh to
poor old Gibbs.)

It hadn't seemed long since we had bade the South African journalists farewell at the end of England's triumphant series the previous summer, but there was still plenty of cud to chew. The exchange rate topped the list of subjects and as the skies grew darker, by way of helping us while away the lost hours, one journalist availed us of his eye-boggling picture library of obese women (I think they were women).

Those educated in the ways of political correctness would probably gasp at the primeval exhibitions in cricket press boxes, but for those of us who spend most of our lives there, the conduct rarely shocks. In fact, I think I remember asking for a copy of one obese-image, a practical request to deter me from excessive pie consumption rather than any post-feminist gesture.

Women do not feature much in cricket boxes around the world. In some places, in fact, they are outnumbered by 100 to none. Still, the wonderfully diverse mix of characters from around the world who are drawn to cricket writing renders the imbalance almost irrelevant. Black, white, smelly, fragrant, lanky, squat, fidgety, still, noisy, silent, fat, rakish, rude, gallant, bright, dense, boarish, oafish, hairy, charming, bald, ugly, downright gorgeous and so it goes on. Each of us, to some degree, requires a level of tolerance and to that end, competitive instincts notwithstanding, it is one of the most tolerant environments to work in.

Having said that, the circuit would be more wholesome were there more women roaming it. We see things men don't and introduce fresh – though not always pertinent – angles which in my experience makes for more diverse conversations and a much more interesting time. A better balance would make one feel less conspicuous and provide relief from the endlessly macho habits. It would be a relief, for instance, to have someone listen rather than talk. It is a relief to have someone admit to fear, shyness or insecurity rather than disguise it with breathtaking arrogance. And it is a relief to have someone bring you a coffee without you asking.

In my World Cup travels, I encountered more than 800 writers from around the world (3,500 media passes were issued in total), four of whom were women, all of them covering England. Inevitably, we talked cricket but it was good to draw the subject out to which of the players would be selected in our Cute Butts XI or Creatures from the Deep XI. It is clear that such conversations unnerved our male counterparts since, they claimed, they were overtly sexist and had no place in such egalitarian company. If all sexist prittle-prattle in cricket press boxes were monitored, I feel confident my corner would require next to no defending.

One of the main challenges as a member of a gender minority in cricket, is to be taken seriously. Imagine sitting next to someone for hours talking about the game and then when something questionable occurs on the field, they lean across you, ignoring you completely, to ask a male colleague what happened.

Whenever I asked a question in a press conference (and it wasn't often) the answer was invariably delivered in a softer, more explanatory vein than if the question had been put by a bloke. It was as if I was unable to understand the essence of the answer without such careful long-winded explanations about how cricket is played.

These practices, which I recognise to be a function of conditioning rather than chauvinism, do little for confidence levels and could explain why so few women have shone in the business of covering cricket. Oh to be treated equally!

HAVING A SEMINAL EXPERIENCE in a shopping mall is not something to be recommended but it happened to me, a few days before World Cup 99, in one of those aircraft hangar-type sport emporiums.

For weeks, my mind had been churning over 25 years' worth of World Cup history and I emerged from a multi-storey pile of books thinking that, like me, the entire world revolved around the orgy of cricket that lay ahead. But it was the stomach that started churning when I suddenly realised in that shop that World Cup cricket was way down the list in the sporting nation's priorities.

The store's entire cricket merchandise, untidily arranged in a dimly lit sub-section at the rear of a cavernous warehouse, amounted to a dozen bats. Actually there were 11. In my shock, I counted them. And that was it. No World Cup promotional material, no enticing offers, not the slightest indication that in a matter of hours, the world's greatest contemporary legends would be descending on these shores to thrill the entire universe with their magical sporting exploits. There was not even a poster of Darren Gough.

By contrast, there was plenty of football paraphernalia. At the tills, excited crowds handed over huge wads of notes for the new England football strip released that week. It was a grotesque sight and I was left pondering the enormity of the task that had fallen to a group of 15 men, selected to revive England's cricketing fortunes, and judging from the pathetic evidence in that shop, to revitalise the British public's woeful interest in the game.

OK, so it was a tough call. England had never won the World Cup. No host country had never won it. Our recent one-day record was iffy but despite that, having conducted dozens of interviews with selectors, players and professional commentators across all nations in preparation, I had become convinced that this time it would be different.

Even though England's preparations had not gone entirely to plan, the squad was organised and had worked harder than ever before so it stood to reason we were about to take the world by storm. Beyond the boundary, the planning and work rate was equally punishing among those of us charged with relaying the action and colour to the rest of the world. With millions of cricket lovers expected to plug in to the official World Cup website for hours at a time, we had had our work cut out to ensure that every single supporter, whoever they were barracking for, had their cravings satisfied.

We (or, to be precise myself and Julian Goode, my editor) had pitched for the rights to host the official World Cup site, on the back of our success with the ECB/MCC's Lords.Org venture and were told three months before the start of the tournament that it was all systems go. Hoorah, though with a staff of two to produce and edit reams of material from 41 matches, I'm not sure we quite realised the enormity of our own task.

Websites lend themselves well to cricket because there is no limit to the entertainment one can present, be it figures, text, pictures (still and moving) and audio. Cricket followers across the world, with their insatiable appetites for news and stats, also seem to be more disposed to the internet than other sports slaves so it was a terrific opportunity for us to capture the global numbers we had anticipated in the original business plan.

Three intensive months of planning, research and design ensued, so by the time the warm-up matches got underway at the start of May, we had a comprehensive database of news, interviews, history, player and team records, venue and ticket details on the menu, all compiled on dark wintry evenings in our hutch at Lord's.

As England limbered up in Sharjah, I was midway through my own preparations for the gruelling seven-week schedule. In the heat of the desert, Alec Stewart and the boys were sizing up Shoaib Akhtar for pace but at a health spa in Surrey, I was peering across a sweltering steam room at another huge prospect. Monica Lewinsky was a fellow guest trying in vain to maintain her anonymity while working off the pounds but her Seppo drawl and ample curves gave her away, much to our infinite fascination.

Alec may not agree but I wouldn't have swapped places for all the tea in Tesco because a) Shoaib is a bit quick for my liking and b) the cigar queen of the White House was compelling, though admittedly unable to shed much light on England's best strategy. Her mind, unlike the rest of us, was focused on non-cricketing matters. Shame really. I felt she had a lot to offer the game.

SO, AFTER ALL THIS DILIGENCE, I was ready and raring to go: 32 matches pencilled in at 14 different venues and a workload the likes of which I had never faced before. My itinerary was, as it turned out, the most arduous of any journalist covering the tournament, involving mad overnight dashes from Nottingham to Taunton, Leeds to Lord's, Cardiff to Manchester, complete with 3D panorama of petrol stations, hotel rooms and press boxes to break up the tarmac.

My brief, put simply, was to get as many cricketers as possible talking expansively into my digital recorder. Not only were there the 174 players to pick on, there was also a giant-size hall of old fame to poke the microphone at as Imran Khan, Sir Vivian Richards, Ian Botham, Jeff Thomson, Martin Crowe, Sunil Gavaskar, Mudassar Nazar, Allan Border and Barry Richards among others flew in to offer their expert commentary. I was then to sort through what they had said using editing software loaded onto the laptop, convert the interviews into useable audio files, provide some explanatory text and send the whole package back to the office for all the world to see or hear.

By the time the first ball was bowled, I was a World Cup bore. I could have told you who did what, when, how and whether it mattered. I would fall into bed at night with blurred visions of Collis King running off the pitch at Lord's in 1979, Winston Davis' seven for 51 against Australia in 1983 or yet another Javed Miandad slice and gallop to send me on my way into the land of nod

The more I researched, the more vivid the images had become. Despite never actually having been to a World Cup fixture, I was easily able to conjure up the atmosphere by reading reports and hearing eye-witness accounts. Talk of massive tightly-packed stadiums created deafening noise; blistering heat – even in England – had the flies buzzing and turbans flagging. Whether it was a traditional English picnic, a Four-n-Twenty pie or a Bombay mix, strong aromas wafted through to complete the picture. In some ways, those heady days of anticipation evoked the best memories.

My World Cup debut at Hove on the first Monday in May, watching South Africa warm up against Sussex (or, rather, attending the obesity exhibition), presented an altogether less exotic picture. Rain clouds and stinky hot dogs served as the opening images of 1999. So much for the brochure ...

The inevitable abandonment at least gave us all time to get some interviews with various South African warriors in the can. In the days preceding, I had travelled to Bristol in search of the West Indians and to Cardiff where the Australians were based: both journeys proved thoroughly worthwhile, not necessarily in the words they offered for the record but in the impressions they gave.

The West Indians struck me as a disparate lot. Sensitive beyond recognition and broody beyond reason. For me, it was obvious from that one session that they had no chance of making the World Cup theirs for the third time.

Australia confused me. Following their Caribbean tour, Steve Waugh looked tired but was relentlessly professional and confident, treating the daftest media questions with respect. "What is your nickname?" one TV journalist asked. "Tugga" came the prosaic rejoinder. "So why's that then?" the idiot continued. It was excruciating.

Other Aussies relished the chance of talking to the press, many of them using the opportunity to advertise the energy that had been in doubt and also their availability for next year's county circuit. That angle was irritating. How come Aussies – and others for that matter – slag off county cricket in one breath then seek a deal with Anyoneshire the next? OK, I know the answer to that one but what I can't fathom is why English clubs use up valuable resources paying these guys to get accustomed to our pitches, players and conditions just so they can chop us up and bung us in the blender when they next turn up to play against us. I must have missed the point somewhere along the line because the practice continues in perpetuity since, it is said, it raises our own domestic standards. But no other nation does it and I suspect they are all sniggering at our naivety behind their glittering trophies.

And so it was that the former Middlesex and incoming Glamorgan all-rounder Jacques Kallis won the first World Cup 99 man of the match award for his decisive exploits against India in the first World Cup fixture proper, though they were, admittedly, small fry compared to the day's big story. The South Africans were sporting earpieces providing a link between the action on the field and the guru in the dressing room. I remember thinking "this can't be right, they must be taking the mickey". I then listened to Sky TV's interview with coach Bob Woolmer who apologised disingenuously if he had upset anyone and I thought "this isn't right: he's taking the mickey". The South Africans' grasp of mind games is on a par with the Australians so it was difficult to understand why they should need or want to resort to such tactics. For the first time, it made me doubt the strength of their famous self-belief and thereafter, for me anyway, Hansie Cronje lost some of his authority. As befits his ranking as one of the most able (and winsome) men in cricket, he has always impressed me, on and off the field, but that one naive move changed my view of him. Despite that, he appeared the most helpful and friendly of all the captains when it came to giving interviews, and by some margin the most desperate to make this World Cup his own. He was so hungry it hurt. His eyes said it all.

I think I got to interview 10 of the 12 captains, either personally or in a press conference, and it was interesting to compare them. How trussed up, pressed for time, defensive and inarticulate the England skipper seemed in comparison to everyone else. There can be no better way of exposing a lack of confidence than a transparently defensive demeanour. Wasim Akram was compelling and since he was the only one to insist on showering and changing before he talked to us, he won my vote for being the most hygiene-aware. I admired his use of the twinkling eye or the withering riposte to maintain control. When he decided he had had enough, he would deliver a cheeky one-liner and sweep out. All the others were given their marching orders by press officers when time was up.

Baby-skippers Alistair Campbell and Stephen Fleming surprised me with their grasp of the soundbite and their manly maturity. The podgy Ranatunga was direct while cleverly evasive. Aminul Islam of Bangladesh impressed me hugely on account of his understanding of websites and the internet (his wife is a computer buff, it transpires). Brian Lara was as I expected. Insincere and unconvincing, a meaningless flow of media-speak shedding next to no light on nothing in particular.

Mohammad Azharuddin was maddening. A serial fidget, he pounced on anything within fiddling distance; twice it happened to be my microphone. He switched it on and off, on and off, fingering it constantly to create interruptions and distortion on the recording.

I encountered writers, four **women.** It was the subject Cute Butts XI from the This **unnerved** counter

more than 800
of whom were
good to draw
out to our
or Creatures
Deep XI.
our male
parts

The New Ball

I took to sitting at the front so I could smack him if he looked like sabotaging another attempt to get Azhar on the website. Thankfully, I never had to resort to such violence. He has such dignity, smacking him would have been inappropriate, though I came close at Taunton where his fidgeting reached new heights after Dravid and Ganguly had carved the Sri Lankan attack to pieces but left him only seven deliveries to play himself into form.

I FELT LIKE SMACKING Steve Waugh too, after he had used the expression "dug deep" for the squillionth time. There must have been a spread-betting book opened on how many times he could repeat it since there was no other plausible explanation. He is short on neither vocabulary nor imagination, as my extensive Steve Waugh World Cup audio collection – comprising hours of his eloquent offerings from that first meeting at Cardiff through eight matches to the final – would indicate. Repetition aside, I never got bored of Waugh.

Although Lance Klusener was man of the tournament, it was Australia's skipper who became the fulcrum of my World Cup universe for his all-round perfection on and off the pitch. A decade ago, I remember a group of us girls were sitting around over a bottle of wine or two discussing whose baby we would have, given the choice (yes, we do that sort of thing!) It was a strictly technical sort of discussion based on gene content rather than any personal interaction and after giving it a lot of thought I plumped for Steve Waugh (though Eric Clapton came a close second). His natural gifts were awesome, despite the unfortunate flat feet, and the list of positive character traits offered a complete recipe for total success. Hunger, confidence, determination and consistency: it was all there. If you were after gutsy, gritty and talented offspring, he promised optimum gene potential. Lucky wife, we all agreed then. Lucky kids, I would say now, having witnessed his brilliant career.

His matchwinning innings against South Africa at Headingley will remain one of the most striking images of the tournament, not just for the sheer magnitude of it but for the tight-lipped expression that screamed "DON'T MESS WITH ME" as he marched out to do battle. What an awesome competitor. (That's two awesomes; one more and you're off – Ed.)

ANOTHER CLEAR feature in the murky maelstrom of memories was again at Headingley but this time in the traffic jam outside, after Pakistan pipped Australia in the group stages. Pakistani supporters indulge their passion in the same way as Pakistan play their cricket – wonderfully flamboyant, uninhibited and noisy, so noisy. On that balmy night in Leeds, they were in ecstasy. As we sat bumper-to-bumper, the horns were blaring, the flags were flying from the car roofs and they were chanting that "Zindaman" chant that was to become more of a theme tune to World Cup 99 than the sqibbish official effort. The atmosphere was electrifying and as I sat there, stationary for well over an hour with handbrake on, I wondered how Lahore must have celebrated in 1992.

But there will be no such whimsical curiosity when it comes to recalling the earth-shattering lowlight. I kept a diary of this tournament, droning into a dictaphone as I travelled the 5,000 interminable miles up and down and across the country, from early morning to even earlier morning. I droned and droned and I droned. But my account of how I felt when England were knocked out is something I will keep forever because it was possibly the darkest cricketing moment I've ever experienced.

On the evidence of their daily and often damning reports, many people think cricket journalists don't care about England's fortunes but that is simply not the case. I remember very clearly the tears in the eyes of one experienced tabloid hack when Mark Ramprakash made his century in Barbados in 1998. It was such an emotional moment; I wish every player had seen the hack in question because, from one brief untempered show of sentiment, they would have understood so much more about how badly English cricket writers want their side to do well, the demands of their jobs notwithstanding.

When play was called off early on that Saturday at Edgbaston because of rain and Zimbabwe had beaten South Africa at Chelmsford, a group of us went out for a curry in Birmingham. We dissected England's performance that day and speculated on the outcome the next, but when Mike Dickson of the *Daily Mail* looked up and said quietly, "They CAN'T lose, can they?", there was such raw distress etched on his face, it silenced the entire table. There was a spooky hush all round as the grim repercussions of an early exit dawned.

They did lose and it reminded me of the day Princess Diana died. Complete and total shock. Saw it in front of me, watched it again on telly, went to the press conference and duly, routinely delivered the goods back to base. But I had to read it in black and white, several times over, before it sunk in. Then the emotions started to surface. The overwhelming sadness soon gave way to anger, not at our lack of talent but at our stupidity in believing that simply winning matches would be enough to see us through. None of us felt that the importance of run rates in this format of the competition had been adequately acknowledged in the England camp. And if it had been, how come it did not translate into any of the game plans in the preceding games. Even now I feel cross about it. Only Adam Hollioake, it eventually transpired, had even thought to bring the subject up (only to be told to put it down again). We were out of the World Cup because we had cocked up on the rules we had written. It was like a Noel Edmonds "Gotcha", only less comical.

AFTER THAT, it became more difficult to get out of bed in the morning, to bother to find out which match was on the schedule that day, to remember we at the World Cup website had an audience that extended throughout the globe, not just across the shires. For a while the whole event became a depressing drudgery, until, that is, the Australians started firing and then, praise be, the juices resumed their flow.

It was always going to be a close contest in that last Super Six match at Headingley. South Africa and Australia are so similar. Rich in reserves and equal in mindset but the Proteas had gained a reputation for bottling it on the big occasions. We all know what happened next, so OK: could they hold their nerve in the semi-final against the same opponents at Edgbaston? Yes, no, yes, no. Yes. Then no. A tie – and a truly spectacular one at that. It is tempting here to rewrite the match report but by now you are probably as familiar with that theatrical finish as you are with The Moment They Thought It Was All Over. The stunned despair in Cronje's eyes at the press conference spoke volumes and will remain with me long after the triumphant grins of the champions lose their gloss.

That drama apart, World Cup 99 will, for me, be remembered

more, sadly, for the hassles and exhaustion than the quality of the cricket. Faced with such a relentless schedule, the unexpected inconveniences on the accommodation front, be it in press boxes (no seats), car parks (no spaces) or hotels (no rooms), became disproportionately preoccupying.

Thank goodness for Tony Pigott, the then chief executive at Sussex CCC, who handed over his office when we were deprived of space in the press box at Hove. And thank goodness for a male colleague who willingly took to an uncomfortably makeshift Z-bed when we finally arrived in Bristol late one night, without a hotel booking. To my eternal gratitude, he insisted I should have the only bed left in town.

It is a disappointing indictment of World Cup 99 that these gentlemanly gestures feature as two of only a handful of fond memories. The others belong, in the main, to Steve Waugh and his genes. ⟐

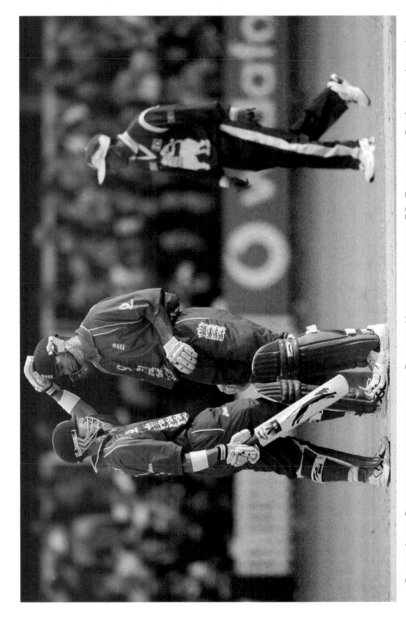

OASIS ALEC STEWART CONGRATULATES GRAEME HICK ON REACHING 50, ENGLAND v SRI LANKA, LORD'S

Blur Darren Gough loses his way, England v Kenya, Canterbury

Mark Steel
XTC In Crowded Houses

Mark Steel writes a weekly column for *The Independent*. He presents Radio 5's sports show *Extra Time* and Radio 4's *The Mark Steel Lecture*. During a World Cup match at Lord's a six from Tom Moody landed in his beer.

Wickedest wicket In a Sheffield pub, the TV was showing the Test match, but the place was heaving, and I was the only one watching. Amid the loud chatter, Warne unforgettably bowled Gatting. No one else cared, and for the next 10 minutes probably thought "why is that loony staring open-mouthed into space?"

Soundest bite "Good batsmen score a century every five Tests." (Geoff Boycott, who averaged a century every 4.96)

Stood in the toilet at Lord's, my thoughts

wandered back to Barbados. In particular, to the row in the Kensington Stand that became so heated it could be heard above the singing and hooting and drinking and whistling and drumming that is the rhythm of a Bridgetown Test.

"I tell ya," screamed one combatant, "Lara is flashy, but Chanderpaul is the better batsman," his whole body lurching forward on the important syllables, like "tell" and "La" and "Chand". But his opponent was the only person in the vicinity who didn't hear, because he was yelling "How can you say dat, how can you say dat?" while waving his arms furiously above his head.

If this had been an English Test ground, they'd have both been dumped outside by the stewards 20 decibels ago. Eventually it reached such a pitch, that even the hands-off police with camp red bands around their peaked caps, and batons tucked neatly into their short-sleeved shirts, meandered across to intervene. This was the first time I'd seen the local officialdom respond to the boisterous spectators in any way. Would there be arrests, brutality, or a polite Caribbean warning to calm down please? One of the coppers tapped the first protagonist on the shoulder, and said crisply, "Ya talking rubbish about Chanderpaul", his body lurching forward on the "rub". Then he walked back to his spot, and the row carried on louder than ever.

The exuberance of the crowd reverberates around the ground,

creating a continuous buzz, the melody to the perennial beat of "ber-da ber-da ber-da peeeep honk" of drums, whistles and horns. A series of people selling things trickle past in sequence. First the apple man, the butt of abuse between overs, especially from the women. "I buy your apples yesterday, they stale," one bellows. "I pick 'em fresh meself," he roars back, and you start to get the idea. Barbadians – or Bajan – cricket crowds have invented their own form of abuse, which contains no Eastenders-style malice or aggression, but is purely abuse for fun.

Other vendors make loud claims for their products that no one is expected to believe. "Last two fishcakes," yells the fishcake man, carrying a huge cardboard box on his shoulder. A punter beckons, and he puts the box on the floor which, as everyone can see, contains five or six hundred fishcakes. He completes the sale of the addictive part-fish, part-doughnut, part-vicious-burning-chilli-object that is a Bajan fishcake. Then he lifts the box back onto his shoulder and screams "last two fishcakes".

At the back is an enormously long bar, stretching from one end of the stand to the other, about one quarter of the perimeter of the entire ground. The bar staff are the only people in the ground who move with any speed, to keep up with the constant demand for rum and coke, and beer. The system transcends all concepts of "the round". You hang around the bar, waving a note, and while waiting, a complete stranger will pour rum into your glass. For someone brought up with the regimented drinking traditions of South London, this is most disconcerting. Your instinct is to snarl, until you realise you'd be saying, "Oy mate, you trying to add to my drink or what? No, hang on, that doesn't sound right. Oy, that's my air you're filling."

The system is genial, labour-saving and egalitarian. If you were skint, no one would notice or mind that you hadn't bought a bottle. Who would pinpoint an individual amongst the crowd, and snap "I've been watching you all day, you haven't bought a round"? It also makes everyone feel part of the crowd, rather than of their own contingent. It's hard not to strike up a conversation with someone when they've just splashed three inches of rum in your glass. And as with any crowd watching sport, one of the main forms of communication is the quiz. "Who's the only man to score a double century in each innings of a first-class match?" "Who was the bowler when Lara overtook Sobers' record?"

"Who is the only man who knew how to bowl out Desmond Haynes – regularly?", I was asked. This seemed an unusual one. And a little arbitrary. After all, who's to say what's regular? Once every eight years is regular. "I don't know," I conceded. "Me" came the answer.

What are you supposed to say when someone says that? I paused for a moment, just in case through my rum-induced stupor I hadn't realised I was talking to Michael Holding. Then I pondered, "I could say 'Fuck me, you bowled Desmond Haynes regularly! Then you are truly an unsung God of the game'." Or I could say "Go on then, prove it. I'll get David Lloyd over here, and let's see if he says 'hello mate, aren't you that bloke who used to bowl Desmond Haynes regularly? I'm glad you were never picked for the Test team, or you'd have taken 2,000 wickets at an average of three'." But I opted for "oh, really", as if he'd told me he was a window cleaner.

He then told me that he'd played a game the previous day, in which he'd scored 50 not out and taken eight wickets for two runs. So whoever scored the two runs should be playing for the West Indies, as they're far superior to Desmond Haynes. Bullshitter.

IF YOU WANT TO WANDER outside for a while, the only bureaucracy is a rubber mark stamped onto the back of your hand, in the style of a student disco. Then you can wander into almost any area of the ground, past an official at the entrance who looks vaguely in the direction of your hand and waves you in. The faintest smudge of newsprint would get you past, unless they could spot a forged stamp mark from 10 yards, while looking in the opposite direction. If only they employed these blokes as ticket inspectors on Connex South Central.

Or you can meander outside to tour the corrugated iron huts that act as stalls selling chicken and rice, rotis, pineapples carved into a corkscrew shape, and coconuts sliced in half with one swipe of a machete. Some of these huts are decorated by stacks of amplifiers, which boom out uninterrupted raga, the bass so loud that the containers for the food jiggle rhythmically across the wooden tables they're perched upon.

Amid the cocktail of noise and emotion, the most disinterested spectator would stand in this crowd and feel that momentous events were happening. Which is why, no matter how much you embrace the drink, the fishcakes, the apples, the noise and the bullshitters, you never miss a ball. The carnival isn't a distraction from the cricket, it's a part of the cricket. Every aspect of the buzz acts in response to the game. During a dogged innings, the rumble takes on a philosophical air, as if the crowd is concentrating in rhythm with the batsman. If Ambrose is roaring in at full pace, the rumble accelerates with him. It feels as if even the bullshitter bullshits twice as fast when Ambrose is bowling. When the spinners are on, he probably tries slower, more restrained bullshits, like "my uncle's the Foreign Secretary". Trapping his victim into thinking "hmmm, well that one might be true", before realising you've been done by his subtle change of flight.

And if a West Indian hits a boundary or takes a wicket, the whole place erupts, not in the uniform cheering of a soccer crowd after a goal, but with everyone playing their full-time role more exuberantly than ever. The drumbeat doubles in pace, the trumpets go into free-form jazz, the arguments become louder than ever, possibly because this incident has resolved it. It seems as if the fishcake man should go up a notch ("Last one") and the bullshitter should go into overdrive ("I am Desmond Haynes").

And this is a knowledgeable crowd, the type that turn up to the last day's play in England. They applaud yorkers, and break off from yelling slogans such as "you can't bat, Stewart", to shout "try Walsh at the other end round the wicket". And they're confidently knowledgeable, so that combined with the uninhibited partying, it's like being surrounded by a crowd of Geoff Boycotts on ecstasy. And it all takes place in glorious unbroken heat, with a group of palm trees just beyond the midwicket boundary.

Occasionally, while soaking up the glorious cameraderie, I pondered where the MCC would have to start, if they took control of the Kensington Oval and tried to reconstruct it in their image. Would they begin by clearing out the huts? Or ban the music first?

Maybe they'd demolish the bar and replace it with a plastic cubbyhole facing away from the play, staffed by one beleaguered teenager, serving lager in plastic beakers at hotel prices. Or they could throw out Fishcake Man, and hand the franchise to a company which sold soggy microwaved sausage rolls for the price of a curry.

It's not just that the authorities are more lenient than over here, and allow you to behave more freely. You're *supposed* to take part like this. You don't watch the event that is a Test match, you *are* the event that is the Test match. Or at least part of one half of the Test match – the crowd.

Which takes a day or so to get used to. At first you find yourself trying to sneak past stewards that are happy to let you past anyway, making you feel like a dog that's been beaten by its previous owner, and still cowers whenever his new owner comes near.

The Caribbean policy ensures that cricket continues to be a game of all the people. On my way to the match each morning I passed a building site, where builders would lean off the scaffolding to yell their predictions. "Lara, he only make 40 today, but Hooper will make 125. Then Ambrose, he bowl out Atherton." A barman opened a conversation one night thus: "Before I serve you, what are the 10 ways a batsman can be out?" What a fantastic country! You have to answer a cricket quiz before you can buy a beer.

The obsession became even more apparent during the next Test in Antigua, which took place while I was still in Barbados. In the towns it's almost impossible to be out of earshot of the radio. In any street, as one fades from behind, another blares from up ahead, from a shop, a cab, a bar or building site. I was in a newsagents when an old woman walked in, screamed "he should've declared", and walked out. Doing my "see the real Barbados" bit, I spent an afternoon in a "rum shop", one of the corrugated iron shacks that line the roads of the poorer areas. An old tramp sat next to me and explained why Atherton gets in trouble with the ball that swings late.

FRAGMENTS OF THESE THOUGHTS passed through my mind, as I stood in that toilet at Lord's. About 150 of us had stood around the truck that served as a bar for the Zimbabwe versus Australia match. Or rather, didn't serve. "That's it," announced the barman, followed by the nightmarish English sound of a shutter ratcheting down in front of alcohol, leaving you helplessly aware of your own insignificance. The incredulous crowd stared for a moment, shrieked, jostled, pleaded and waved money in the air. Then we resigned ourselves and turned disconsolately away, like the unemployed dockers rejected for work in *On the Waterfront*.

All the bars were shut, we were told, for the next three hours. But that wasn't quite true. Just to the left the champagne bar was rollicking merrily along, its cheapest product a bottle of the champagne you don't get in Sainsbury's, for fifty-four quid. I wonder if there was a meeting to discuss the price at which it was deemed safe to allow people to drink in the afternoon. With members proposing "Whereas the common lager drinker is likely to be sick and wipe themselves with a tissue, the chap who can afford fifty-four pounds a bottle will get paralytic with the demeanour appropriate to the home of cricket; dabbing themselves with a silk handkerchief. Or better still, getting their cleaner to do it for them."

That's when I sloped off to the toilet, and stood between a Zimbabwean and an Australian, each united in their bewilderment at this prohibition policy. Suddenly, like a German liberal, I felt guilty for the crimes of my country. "May I take this opportunity," I announced, "to apologise on behalf of my ridiculous shitty nation." They both assured me it wasn't my fault.

By itself this rule is hardly the planet's worst example of repression. But it comes on top of so many other petty restrictions that make the common spectator at English grounds feel they're an unwanted nuisance, an intruder, as if you're six and you've visited your Dad's office. "No you can't bring flags. Give me that klaxon at once. What have I told you about making rhythmic carnival-like noises? You will not buy your ticket on the day, you'll get it by credit card because I said so. Right, I warned you about making a noise at the Tavern, now I'm going to shut it down and concrete it over."

So how has this disparity come about? One answer is that frugal austerity is the English way; we're just not a carnival sort of nation. Maybe there's some truth in this. An account of a tour of the West Indies in 1895, written by AF Somerset, began: "A batsman who stops a yorker evokes a yell, which in England would not be given for a hit out of the ground. When that comes off, a large part of the crowd spring on to the ground, throw their hands and umbrellas in the air, perform fantastic dances, and some of them are occasionally arrested by the police."

For stopping a yorker! That must have been knackering. If you were in the crowd, you'd have been praying for an over of long hops drifting gently down the leg side, just for a rest.

The noise of the crowd during the early tours was so great, that captains carried whistles to attract their fielders' attention, as shouting couldn't be heard. But to suggest culture as the only reason for the different types of crowd, is to excuse those responsible for compounding the image of English cricket as a sad pastime for retired eccentrics. The rulers of the English game would happily agree that we're different, concluding that nothing can be done about it. I met Tim Lamb shortly after that 1998 series in the West Indies, and enthused to him about watching cricket there. This just went to show, he replied, that the marvellous thing about cricket, is it suits either environment. "We enjoy watching it in our traditional way," he added, "while they prefer it with all their reggae music."

The funniest word in that sentence was "reggae", especially when pronounced in a clipped middle-class accent, and spoken with inverted commas, as awkward as an old aunty trying to sound modern by saying the latest Richard Clayderman album is "wicked". But the most important word was "we". Who is we? The English? If the atmosphere at English grounds was as vibrant as in the West Indies, would the majority of English cricket followers mourn the days of watching it in our traditional way?

The question is not entirely hypothetical, because not long ago the spirit of the West Indian crowd was to be found at English Test grounds. The accessories – fishcakes, laid back cricket-loving coppers, sunshine, palm trees and "reggae" music – may not have been present, but the essence of the atmosphere was. England's home series against the West Indies from 1963 to 1976 are among the most memorable of recent history, not just for the standard of play, but because the huge West Indian contingent implanted the Caribbean spirit into English grounds.

They sang and hooted and drank and whistled and drummed.

The New Ball

They danced to fanfares as first Sobers then Lloyd then Richards destroyed the English bowling. And at The Oval, when Richards reached his second double century of the 1976 series, a chant of "grovel Greig grovel" tunefully flowed round the ground, with many English fans joining in, as a retort to Tony Greig's comment before the series that he would "make them grovel". Richards and Co, that is. One West Indian became a celebrity for a summer, for applying all this passion to Geoff Boycott, screaming witticisms of adoration at every opportunity to his hero. And this was in the days before post-modern irony.

With few exceptions we, the English, loved it. The millions who followed it on radio or television seemed just as enthusiastic. In my small, all-white town of Swanley, people with little interest in cricket acknowledged that a day at the Test would be a great day out. And this was when racism was at its postwar height, shortly before the National Front received 100,000 votes in the GLC elections.

The attitude towards the West Indian crowd transcended the prejudices of the day: racism, and the one that can seem even harder to crack, that cricket is a tedious game for stuffy colonels.

BUT ONE GROUP, ANOTHER "WE", disapproved. The noise wasn't in keeping with the dusty reverence expected of a crowd at Lord's. How can one enjoy a champagne picnic with that racket going on? One by one the restrictions were put in place. No hooters, no flags, no standing in groups, no Tavern (too noisy), no drums, no turning up on the day, and so on. Over the next 20 years the authorities succeeded in preventing the West Indian supporters from injecting their spirit into the English game. Better than that, they prevented them from coming at all. Now the most enthusiastic set of cricket supporters feels disinclined to attend matches in this country.

I know several West Indians who say the specific reason they no longer go to Tests in England, is the curtailment of all that is integral to watching the game in their homelands. It must be similar to English football fans living in a country where you could attend matches but weren't allowed to chant or sing, and where it was expected that you watched in polite silence. Most would eventually decide not to bother going.

At Lord's
I came across
a **jazz** outfit
reminiscent
of the acts you
knew would
come **last** on
Opportunity
Knocks

The New Ball

And the stifling attitude isn't just aimed at West Indians. Tim Lamb described the World Cup as the best and most successful ever. By what criteria? The numbers attending? Clearly not. The enthusiasm created in the host nation? Hardly. How did the England and Wales Cricket Board exploit the opening fixture, between England and champions Sri Lanka at Lord's, as a platform for selling the game? Where were the bands, the processions, the celebration of a world event? It would be a lie to say there was no music. Touring the ground at the lunch interval, I came across a three-piece trad jazz outfit, wearing white suits and boaters, playing songs like *You Are My Sunshine*, reminiscent of the acts that you knew would come last on *Opportunity Knocks*.

To be honest I quite enjoyed them. If I'd stumbled across them at a village fete, I'd have spent a pleasant five minutes humming along. But this was the opening bloody ceremony! What marketing wizard with their finger on the pulse of youth culture came up with that stroke of genius? I must have missed the other elements of the opening celebrations, which were probably a bloke from Wiltshire displaying antique cuckoo clocks, and a lecture on Disraeli by Norman St. John Stevas.

Compare this to the opening ceremony of the 1996 World Cup, as described by Mike Marqusee:

> Famous artists were booked to sing and dance. India's Miss Universe would descend from a helicopter inside a laser-generated cricket ball. The star of the show would be a thirteen-minute laser presentation, dubbed 'Wills batsman', depicting the rise of the cricketer from the urban alleyway to the Test arena. This would be followed by an eighteen-minute fireworks display designed by a French specialist, involving 3.5 tonnes of gunpowder.

They never had no trombones though, did they? Which makes ours the best organised World Cup ever.

Almost every journalist and commentator agreed that one of the highlights of the competition was the enthusiasm of the Asian cricket fans. Yet far from being encouraged, this enthusiasm could only make an appearance despite the best efforts of the authorities. Why was no effort made to involve the enormous East London Bengali community? Why was there no Sri Lankan music at the opening match? Where was the encouragement to schools with large numbers of Indian and Pakistani children to become involved in the competition? What arrogance to sell all the tickets to the final before anyone knew who the finalists would be, and deal with complaints by stating that Australians and Pakistanis deserve no extra tickets, "just because their teams are in the final".

Occasionally a blast of reality permeates its way into the estranged world of the English cricket authorities, and they concede a reform or two. Although even this requires a major internal upheaval. The most famous example is the MCC finally being dragged kicking and screaming into allowing women to become members which, for some members, was tantamount to inviting The Prodigy to play at the annual dinner and dance.

During the World Cup they finally, grudgingly, relaxed the restrictions on flags and musical instruments (although the music was re-banned for the latter stages). However, the restrictions on alcohol were tightened further. These tiny reforms are like the reforms offered by a dying, crisis-ridden civilisation shortly before it's swept away. The MCC and ECB are like the Confederate states in the last days of the civil war. They promise to reform their ways with meaningless gestures, giving counties nicknames like Kent Spitfire. But they're incapable of understanding that what's required is an overhaul that would remove their whole system.

Imagine a body that not only permitted, but positively encouraged a carnival spirit throughout the game. That incorporated the Asian and West Indian communities into the national structure. That aimed to create an atmosphere at matches so exciting that people who didn't understand cricket still went. That built stands with a bar, with standing areas from which you can see the play.

Imagine the enormous effort that goes into attracting corporate bookings for Test matches. Market research groups, teams of staff and marketing experts, mailshots, glossy brochures and databases are all in place to capture every business opportunity. Imagine if a similar effort went into promoting the game to attracting working-class youth, and creating an environment in which they'd feel at ease.

To suggest these things, all of which are fundamental parts of the game in the West Indies, is to realise how far adrift the English authorities are. What other institution, apart from English cricket, would appoint as the overseer of a radical overhaul a Lord, whose main qualification is that he's a cricket-loving supermarket millionaire? Is there any organisation, apart from English cricket, which would take seriously a man like Lieutenant Colonel Stephenson, let alone make him secretary of the ICC?

The lieutenant may well be a "decent chap", whatever that is, but he's a living caricature of all that's absurd about the English cricket hierarchy. He rigorously opposed the admission of women into the MCC, and applied for the job of club secretary (and hence ICC secretary) because, he told me in a radio interview, he fancied a change from the army, and his qualifications were "none whatsoever". Yet when I referred to this in the *Guardian*, Mike Selvey wrote an angry retort in defence of Stephenson, demanding why it was that "people who know nothing about the game feel they can write about it". Stephenson, he said, was a reformer.

SO NOT ONLY DO THEY FAIL to attract a new generation of English cricket fans; they alienate people who were already fans before coming to this country, and turn them away as well.

And, like the Confederates, they have no concept of the extent of the decay. Because they don't inhabit working-class communities, they don't see the decline in interest over the last 30 years. Now we're officially (sort of) the worst in the world. But the official response is that although this is a little disappointing, we shouldn't worry too much as the Under-19s did rather well, and those charts can't be taken seriously. Atlanta is burning, but not to worry – we all know we're better than silly countries like Sri Lanka and New Zealand and Zimbabwe really. Which allows them to pretend that nothing much is wrong, nothing that can't be sorted with another inquiry or two and a fiddle with the league structure.

But the ever deepening problem is the image of the game, sustained by the Lords and lieutenants, and the corporate boxes that remain irritatingly empty for the hour after lunch, even at the World Cup final. It's an image confirmed with every additional petty restriction.

"I couldn't believe it," a friend told me when he received his ticket for the Oval Test, the first day's cricket he'd ever been to. "A notice came with the ticket saying 'you are only permitted to bring two tins of beer into the ground'. I'd like to commission a brewery to make me two giant tins holding 10 gallons each and say 'what are you going to do about that?'" To the English fan, the game is like a wayward brother, or a crazy friend like Robert De Niro in *Mean Streets*, that you find yourself constantly having to apologise for.

Why else would the attitude to the game be so different here and in the West Indies? Here, seen by most people as archaic and dull, whereas to suggest that in the Caribbean would appear ridiculous. It can't be the game itself, which is played by the same rules in both places. It can only be the crowd. In one case static, mistrusted and restricted by countless rules, in the other flamboyant, proud, exuberant and communal.

Which is why West Indies cricket created the calypso, a concept which in English cricket would be unimaginable. How would it go?

We don't wave flags
Or make a sound
Or we'll be evicted from
The cricket ground.
We see corporate boxes
And the MCC
And England lose by an innings and 43.

Cricket English cricket
At Lord's where we play it.
We politely lose our wicket
Unless rain comes to delay it. ◗

SCATTERED ALAN MULLALLY'S PRONE STUMPS SIGNAL THE HOSTS' DEMISE AT EDGBASTON

SHATTERED STEWIE AND BUMBLE, EDGBASTON

Paul Weaver
Amateur Hour

Paul Weaver entered journalism
in Brighton in 1970 after winning
a BBC short story competition.
Worked for Hayters, *Southend
Evening Echo* (Provincial and
Regional Sports Reporter of the
Year, 1976), Westminster Press,
News of the World, *Mirror*,
Today, *Sunday Telegraph* and,
since 1992, the *Guardian*. A club
cricketer of resolute ordinariness,
his prize possession is a yellowing
snippet from the *Southend Standard*
explaining how he top-scored for
Southchurch Seconds, with 18,
before taking six wickets. The
headline is "Viva Weaver".

Wickedest wicket
BA Richards b Snow 42, Sussex v
Hampshire, Hove, 1973. Richards
is putting the acting Sussex captain
to the sword. Snow pitches one up,
it swings in late before cutting
away to flatten the off-stump.
Richards raises his right arm, a
great champion saluting another.

Soundest bite "The Bunburys
will be playing a Winston Davis XI
at Finedon, near Welling-borough,
on May 23. It won't rain. I fixed
it." (David English does his bit for
Winston Davis, 1999.)

Those who mock or mourn English cricket play a
strange, amnesiac trick on themselves. Mentally, they burn all their
Wisdens and choose to forget that the country that gave the game
to the world usually perform like a bunch of duffers when it comes
to putting on a show themselves.

England played in the first Test match ever played, against
Australia in Melbourne in 1877. They lost. They were routed by
the scarcely remembered Australian left-armer Tom Kendall, who
took eight wickets. They have been losing ever since, their flannels
fluttering like flags of truce on many a foreign field. Only once, in
the Fifties, can it be said with any certainty that England had the
best team in the world. Even then, when the side of May, Cowdrey,
Graveney, Evans, Trueman, Statham, Laker, Lock et al went to
Australia for the Ashes series of 1958-59, they were routed 4–1.

England have only fitfully been much good at playing cricket.
The game has come to resemble just one of a number of ingenious
British inventions, thought up over here but under-resourced and
ultimately developed abroad. England, in fact, does not have a
particularly good record in team games generally. Even in football,
vaunted football, the opiate of the masses, the national team have
picked up just one meaningful pot in their entire history, the World
Cup of 1966. Sporting success, traditionally, has been provided by
the potty obsessive, the driven eccentric: the golfer, jockey, racing
driver, boxer, squash player, marksman or swimmer. Even so, what

happened to English cricket in the summer of 1999 was a humilation that undercut all previous embarrassments. And that is really saying something. It was the year the summer game became a giggle-fest, when even the game's most ardent supporters were found tittering nervously, if only to keep the tears at bay.

For some years cricket, along with the Royal Family, had outscored *Eastenders* and Corrie as the nation's favourite soap. But now it was a sitcom. A stand-up's touchstone for guaranteed mirth. The game declined so sharply it was as if it had taken a ride in Disneyworld's Splash Mountain.

Hosting the World Cup for the fourth time, England fell splat on their faces at the first hurdle. In 1975 they had at least breezed through their group and made it to the semi-final; in 1979 they reached the final; in 1983 they again made the semis, where they were beaten by India, the winners of the tournament. Even away, in Calcutta in 1987 and in Melbourne in 1992, they had reached the final. Now, the carnival was over before it had started, before even the official World Cup song had been released. Despite winning the toss five times out of five they failed to make the top three of Group A and so did not qualify for the Super Six stage. A tournament undersold, initially, by the organisers, because they could not find the sponsors to provide the advertising and marketing money, was ultimately sold short by the players.

Worse was to follow. After the World Cup England played New Zealand in a four-Test series. This, in itself, was a crass piece of scheduling by the men at Lord's. Even if the World Cup had captured the imagination – and it did not, at least at first, in a cold, damp, underachieving summer – New Zealand would have represented something of an anti-climax, a small, starless country with little box-office appeal. It did not work out that way. New Zealand outplayed England from first to last. They won the series 2-1 but it should have been 3-1 and it might easily have been 4-0. England had lost at home to New Zealand before, but only once, and then to the side that boasted Martin Crowe's batting and Richard Hadlee's rhythm method back in 1986. The 1999 Kiwis were less gifted, even though Chris Cairns's performances at last matched his prodigious gifts.

Oh, and there was something else. England became the worst cricket team in the world. The *Wisden* World Championship, unofficial and flawed in its reasoning, had nevertheless won a wide following since it was devised in 1996. Then, England were sixth, behind the superpowers but at least ahead of Sri Lanka, Zimbabwe and New Zealand. This was a new low. The English cricket follower had come to resemble one of those awful motorway rubber-neckers where the ambulance cannot get through because the path is blocked by all those who stop and ogle at the mangled wreckage.

A number of pile-ups have littered the English game. The 4-0 home defeat against Australia in 1989 for one. The successive "blackwashes" at the hands of West Indies in 1984 and 1985-86 for two more. The time, in 1988, when they employed four captains in the series against West Indies, not counting Derek Pringle, who became the fifth when the injured Graham Gooch left the field. The shambles of the 1996 World Cup is still a fresh, aching memory. Some argued that last place flattered England. After all, they seldom visit the subcontinent, the most demanding tour for any cricket team. They last went to India and Sri Lanka seven years ago and have not returned to Pakistan since the controversial tour of 1987-88.

England were bottom. Bottom, like the weaver in *A Midsummer Night's Dream* who wore an ass's head. England became the target for worldwide ridicule. One national newspaper even did a spoof reconstruction of the cremation of the game that led to the creation of the Ashes more than a century before. The accrued criticism hardly helped. Gerald Ratner, the infamous jeweller who told his customers that his wares were rubbish, soon convinced his market. Similarly, English cricketers, not particularly good in the first place, came to believe that they were even worse than they were. As the summer progressed they became increasingly introverted, insecure and fragmented.

Even their best players became casualties, literally in the case of the injured Darren Gough. Mark Ramprakash had been England's best batsman in Australia the previous winter but he was dropped for the tour to South Africa because the pressure got to him and he misbehaved too often in the dressing room. A weary Graham Thorpe, never a happy tourist, opted to take the winter off.

The New Ball

SO WHAT REALLY IS WRONG with English cricket? It is a question that has defeated players, officials, intellectuals and sociologists, and one best addressed in private in a darkened room with a good bottle.

There is no shortage of contributory factors. The decline of the game in state schools is one, perhaps the biggest. The game in this country still has an unnatural reliance on public schools, with their superior facilities and pitches, to provide players of international standard.

Poor pitches, flattering bowlers and undermining the batsmen's confidence, is another reason. In the view of the former England opener Tim Robinson, newly retired after two decades on the circuit, they are the worst he has ever encountered. Sometimes "result" pitches are deliberately prepared. But there is also a sense that the dedicated, devoted, timeless groundsman, with the smiling, berry-brown face, is receding into history. His is largely a lost art.

Then there is the climate. The most exotic flora and fauna can be found in warmer climes and it seems that the same thing applies to cricketers. A player brought up with the sun on his back and operating on a hard, true surface surely has an advantage over his English counterpart. At least, his development is likely to be more rapid. But it has ever been thus.

The system itself is deeply flawed. Put simply, there are far too many cricketers playing too much cricket. The talent is too thinly spread. In Australia, for example, there was much heated debate before Tasmania became the sixth state in the Sheffield Shield. In England there are 18 first-class counties and around 400 professional players. There is no quality control. There is also too much one-day cricket. But when the England and Wales Cricket Board sent the Benson and Hedges Cup to the knacker's yard it soon won a reprieve from the selfish, parochial, money-minded counties. The B&H will return in all its old glory next season.

The ECB, essentially, is made up by the counties. Anything passed by a committee at Lord's can be, and often is, vetoed by the First-Class Forum. So the chairman of the board, the grocer Lord MacLaurin, lamentable though he has proved to be, can hardly take all the blame. The counties should relinquish some of their power, but it is a little like asking chocolates to vote for Easter. In view of the fact that county cricket is not well supported there is a sound argument that it should exist purely to further the interests of the national side. After all, counties only survive through their annual share-out from Lord's, ie the profits from Tests and one-day internationals.

Last season the standard of county cricket was lower than anybody could remember. This has nothing to do with the sentimental, nostalgic attatchment to a bygone age; there was a marked decline in playing standards when compared with the very season before. Even Graham Gooch, the yeoman champion of the county game, was in a despairing mood by the end of the season, and not only because he had lost his job as a Test selector. Gooch is not only the most prolific England batsman in Test history. He has also scored more runs in top-class cricket (65,928) than anyone the game has seen, Jack Hobbs included, so his views are worth listening to. He said:

> The players we chose for England over the past couple of years were the best available, given their performances in the domestic game. So what really worries me is the ability level in county cricket, because it plainly isn't high enough. Raising the standard of the domestic game is paramount but we just seem to be going round in circles.
>
> If the people who control the game – and that's the 18 counties the way things are – really want to have a strong Test side, everything else has to be designed to bring that about. Yet we have had several instances down the years when changes, possibly improvements, have been passed through all the committees, then been voted down when it came to the crunch. That gets us nowhere and it makes other countries laugh at us.

It is almost 20 years since the giant South African fast bowler Garth Le Roux told me: "If you had to design a system to produce mediocre cricketers you could not do better than the county championship. You are playing, or travelling, all the time. Usually you are carrying an injury, or at least a twinge or two. Some mornings you wake up strong and feel like charging in. Other mornings, you just go through the motions, not because you are lazy, or without heart, but because your body simply will not allow you any more effort." Since then matters have got worse. Much worse.

The gap between county and Test cricket grows ever wider. Until this can be closed there is an urgent need for an intermediate stage, regional cricket perhaps, in which the best players in the land can escape from the dross that pulls them down. The present system has given birth to the worst sort of county cricketer, curmudgeonly, grimly protective, unhelpful to younger players, who they perceive as a threat to their living, and resistant to change.

THOSE WITH AN EYE AND AN EAR for a morality play might have been attracted by the match between Middlesex and Surrey at Lord's, in the penultimate round of championship fixtures in early September. Any meeting between these two London monoliths has a certain resonance and evokes memories of ancient battles. The clubs have won 26 championships between them, and on 16 of those occasions the prize has gone to The Oval. In the modern era, however, Middlesex have had the better of it. Between the stretched bookends of Surrey's last two championship successes, in 1971 and 1999, Middlesex gleefully filled the void. In that time they won six championships, two Gillette Cups, two NatWest Trophies, two B&H Cups and a Sunday League. The side that won the championship and Gillette Cup double in 1980, as well as finishing third in the Sunday League and reaching the semi-finals of the B & H, was considered one of the best to represent the county.

By the middle Nineties, however, that side had creaked to a standstill. John Emburey had departed, their insatiable Henry VIII lookalike Mike Gatting had lost his appetite, for making runs at least, and too much was being asked of the gallant Boxer, the permanently weary-looking Gus Fraser. The club turned to one of their more enlightened committeemen, the former England wicketkeeper Paul Downton, who came up with an inspired idea. The Australian John Buchanan would replace Don Bennett, retiring after almost half a century at Lord's including three decades as coach, for the 1998 season. Buchanan, though, was given a rough ride. A number of the most senior players, including Gatting, Keith Brown, the captain

Mark Ramprakash and the second XI coach Ian Gould, did not go along with the Australian's revolutionary new ways.

Ramprakash proved to be a poor captain. But he still wanted the absolute power enjoyed by more successful leaders, Gatting and Mike Brearley, before him. The players, meanwhile, were unwilling to devote more time to match preparation, as Buchanan requested. It did not matter that Buchanan had brought unprecedented success to Queensland in the Sheffield Shield, and soon after the World Cup was shortlisted to become the new coach to the national side. Far more important than that, at least for the Middlesex dressing room, was that the cosy mediocrity of county cricket should be maintained. If the club had anything about them they would have backed Buchanan and got rid of the senior players who did not go along with his methods. Instead, they let him go. Fraser, to his credit, almost left because of this.

And so we come to Lord's, the following September. The sun is pale and low. Middlesex are even paler and more lowly. As their bowlers are torn apart by Alistair Brown and Adam Hollioake, the new Middlesex coach, Gatting of course, can be seen pacing the dressing room and balcony in frustration. The county's place in the second division has been confirmed.

It is tempting to paint Gatting in the dark colours of the stage villain, but this would be unfair. This was an outstanding player. A generous one, too, and a captain who led by vivid example. In the end, though, he became part of the rotten system, playing on into his 42nd year before looking around for another job in the same jaded, ineffectual workhouse. He played on until he became an ordinary player, a time-server, the curse of the domestic game. Having had a vast benefit in 1988, worth £205,000, he played on and was granted a second benefit, or testimonial, in 1996. If this was the path of a fundamentally decent man, and an unselfish cricketer, what about the selfish ones?

MEANWHILE, ENGLAND CONTINUE to produce the world's best age-group players. They won the World Youth Cup in South Africa two years ago. But the saddest conversation I had last summer was with the Under-19 coach Tim Boon. "I just wish I could hang on to these players for a little longer," he said. " Instead they go back to their counties and fall into bad habits." Dermot Reeve, who captained Warwickshire to six pieces of silver in three seasons, including a near clean sweep of the four domestic trophies in 1994, is a bright, lateral thinker who feels that the perceived strength of the English game is really its essential weakness: professionalism.

> I don't think it is a particularly good thing that when a batsman goes out there he knows he is playing for his mortgage. It makes him feel threatened, insecure and negative. Why is it that players from other countries always seem more up for it? I think it has to do with the fact that in Australia, for example, Shield players have other jobs, working as teachers, or in banks. That helps them play cricket with more freedom, passion and fun.
>
> In this country we also need to do a lot of work on the players' self-esteem. We have to create the right environment for him, make him happier, more assertive and less sensitive to criticism. We need to make him happier with himself and with his profession.

ALL THIS NAVEL-GAZING and self-flagellation seemed a long way away when the World Cup was launched back in May. England were not very good at Test cricket and knew it. Test matches are won by fast bowlers, wrist-spinners, unconventional finger spinners and, just occasionally, batsmen of genius, such as Brian Lara and Sachin Tendulkar. The England cricket team have none of these jewels. But in one-day cricket they had a grim professionalism and in six World Cups only the West Indies, just, had won more matches. So when the seventh tournament got under way there was a feeling that England would certainly reach the Super Six, secondary stage, and probably the semi-finals.

The World Cup, despite itself, was a qualified success. There were fears that it might have been stillborn when it was delivered into the chill of an English spring, choking on the coloured smoke that masked that laughable opening ceremony at Lord's. Tony Blair was there to open the affair but his microphone didn't work. Ultimately, however, the weather warmed up and Pakistan, Australia, India and South Africa played some outstanding cricket as it became

Sport matters less in **England.** There is a pervading sense of ennui, of **distraction**

increasingly clear that one-day cricket would be the future of the globally marketed game and a colourful spectacle that could match almost any other sport.

England, too, looked as good as anyone in the opening stages. On that opening day, when it seemed that nothing would go right, they thumped the holders Sri Lanka, winning by eight wickets as Alec Stewart and Graeme Hick both struck form. In their second match, against Kenya at Canterbury, they went one better, losing just one wicket as they sauntered to victory with 11 overs to spare. Hick and Nasser Hussain were the stars, although some questioned the choice of the very conservative Canterbury as a venue. There was one delicious moment when an excited spectator started waving with an old-style football rattle. Behind him, an irritated, elderly gentleman said: "Oh do sit down and be quiet!"

Even when England were beaten by South Africa at The Oval the disappointment was only so-so. South Africa were meant to win, after all, though not quite so easily as this. Then England faced Zimbabwe at Trent Bridge. They only had to win to qualify, or so everybody thought. Win they did, and emphatically, cruising home by seven wickets with almost a dozen overs remaining. Hussain and Thorpe led the way.

And so to Birmingham where, on May 29, England faced India in their final group match. The result was surely academic. Then grave news swept the land from Chelmsford, where Zimbabwe had beaten South Africa for the first time in their history. Suddenly, England had to beat India to qualify. They failed with some style. For the fifth time Stewart won the toss but his decision to bowl, in ideal batting conditions, was both defensive and perverse. England's fifth bowler, a dodgy combination of Andrew Flintoff and Adam Hollioake, went for 62 in 10 overs, but India's 232 for eight did not look beyond reach.

It did when the little rated Debashish Mohanty took two wickets in as many (legal) balls. And what wickets! He dismissed Stewart and Hick, bowling a wide in between. As the umpires dithered about the weather Hussain was bowled by Saurav Ganguly. England had scored 73 for three from 20.3 overs and then the rain fell. Then came the shocking bulletin from Chelmsford.

When play resumed on the Sunday the pressure on the England batsmen was intense and they did not respond particularly well. Crucially, Thorpe, whose touch had looked sure, was soon lbw to Javagal Srinath, although it looked as though the ball would have gone down the leg side. Neil Fairbrother looked capable of saving the day but support was negligible. Flintoff, paying for a lack of experience, lifted Anil Kumble for one vast six but then perished lbw to the same bowler, as so many batsmen have. Hollioake swung desperately across the line and then David Lloyd knew that his final game as England coach would be a miserable one.

England were certainly unfortunate. They could not have expected Zimbabwe, even with an inspired Neil Johnson, to defeat South Africa. Neither could they have anticipated the same team overcoming India at Grace Road, where Henry Olonga recovered from two truly awful spells to bowl one, single, inspired over, claiming three wickets. India, missing Tendulkar, who had flown home for his father's funeral, were beaten by three runs. England could also argue that if the rain that interrupted their game against India had washed out the match, and there was no result, they would have progressed. The point was also made that their opening victories were so one-sided that their middle-order batsmen were denied the time in the middle they needed to prepare themselves for the pressure that Edgbaston presented. But there was another reason for England's downfall. They concentrated on winning their matches, one by one. There is little wrong with this football-style philosophy, you may think. But they failed to read the small print. They did not realise the crucial importance of their run-rate until it was too late.

The South Africa bowlers badly damaged their cause at Kennington but they had the chance to boost their rate against Sri Lanka and Kenya and, most clearly, against Zimbabwe, when the last nine runs filled five long overs. Instead of sending in Flintoff, in an effort to win the match and boost the run rate with a flurry of shots, Fairbrother was sent in with the instructions from one selector to "have a net". To his credit Hollioake, and the England scorer, Jack Foley, realised the danger and spoke up. But nobody listened.

THIS, PERHAPS, IS THE MOST EXASPERATING thing of all about English cricket. The fact that we invented the game does not give us a God-given right to trample all over our colonial cousins. But surely it gives us the right to expect not to be out-thought and outwitted at every turn. If we don't have the technique we should at least have the theory.

There was a similar shortfall of grey matter when the Test series got underway. Hussain, a natural captain, replaced Stewart, a wonderful, combative cricketer but a skipper fit only to tread the deck of HMS Troutbridge. Lloyd, who had done his noble best as coach, was also replaced. So far so good. There was even a recall for Phil Tufnell and Andy Caddick. In the past the selectors had afforded themselves the curious luxury of dispensing with a number of their best players. At this stage, though, Hick should have returned. When he did come back, to meet desperate demands, he was once again placed under intense pressure, which he was unable to respond to. Hick will never be forgiven for failing to live up to outlandish expectations, and for not being entirely English. For the past half-dozen years, however, he has been a Test-class batsman, averaging better than Gatting, much better than Ramprakash and producing figures to rival those of Hussain and Mike Atherton.

England's outstanding player was a Kiwi, Caddick. Not one Englishman scored a century in the four Tests; the highest score came courtesy of Alex Tudor, a fast bowler. New Zealand, with much deeper batting, scored three hundreds and made seven further fifties against England's five. The worrying aspect, however, was that, man for man, England appeared to have the better cricketers.

AND HERE WE HAVE THE CRUX OF IT. Suppose, just suppose, that Sunday League cricket and poor pitches and bonus points and the four-day game and two divisions all worked and we actually did produce better cricketers than the Australians. Well, it still wouldn't be enough. England would still lose. For the simple reason that playing for his country does not mean the same thing to an Englishman that it means to an Australian or a New Zealander. For them, and West Indians and Indians and South Africans, it means everything, and even more when they can put one over on the ancient enemy. England is still suffering from post-colonial fall-out.

But there is something else besides. Sport matters less in England. There is a pervading sense of ennui, of distraction, that is difficult to overcome in an affluent, middle-class country. You can change the captain and the coach – and England have had four of each in the past seven years – but it will make little difference. Four-day county cricket has made little difference and two divisions looks an unlikely panacea. The very environment in which they and the players operate is badly in need of a makeover.

The answer may well be to return to the ridiculed days of the amateur. Remember the announcer at Lord's in the late Fifties? "There is one correction to your scorecard. In the Middlesex team FJ Titmus should read Titmus,FJ." Only the amateur had his initials before his name. There is, however, as Reeve suggested, much to be said for the approach of the unprofessional. Some counties are already cutting their staffs from around 30 to something nearer 20. Why not cut them back to 10 or a dozen and top up with the best league and club players. It is, perhaps, time for shock therapy.

Second XI cricket, rendered useless because of the dire quality of pitches, could be done away with altogether. The feudal system of benefits, which is nothing more than highly organised begging, would also be scrapped. These dozen or so professionals would be paid considerably more than they receive now and would be employed the year round. But they would have to produce or their short-term contract would be cancelled. It would concentrate the mind, even though those youngsters attracted to the fame and money of football will never be recalled. It is a chastening thought that if Denis Compton had been born 40 years later he would probably have never played cricket, even if he had wanted to.

Going back to separate dressing rooms for amateurs and professionals might be overdoing it. But the time has come for a rather different discrimination, one between those who perform and those who do not. Until then it might be merciful if England were excused games. 🌑

FRUITFUL KIWI (I) GEOFF ALLOTT GIVES HIMSELF SOME BREATHING SPACE

FRUITFUL KIWI (II) SIR RICHARD HADLEE (RIGHT) WITH GORDON GREENIDGE, CHELMSFORD

Graeme Wright

Beyond The Crowe Road

Graeme Wright, New Zealand-born editor of *Wisden* from 1986 to 1992, came to England in his mid-twenties and worked in publishing before becoming a freelance writer and editor. His books include *Where do I go from here*, written with George Best, and the highly-acclaimed *Betrayal: The Struggle for Cricket's Soul*.

Wickedest wicket Roger Harper's pick-up and throw to run out Graham Gooch in the MCC Bicentenary Match, Lord's, 1987. Cricket's equivalent of a Beckham free-kick or Clint defending his mule's honour.

Soundest bite "There is no reason why, in a country where it is often impossible to have building work done or a motor car serviced properly, its sporting tradesmen should perform any better." (*Wisden*, 1989)

No disputing it. The Poms take the biscuit. Rich Tea,
naturally. They eat our New Zealand lamb and expect our Kiwi
cricketers to go like sheep to the slaughter. Without so much of a
murmur, of course. Then when it all goes wrong – the plot, that is
– the Pommy press blame their own team for being beaten by an outfit
they couldn't quite accept as a pretty useful sum of its parts. You
couldn't hear the silence of the lambs for the bleating of the Brits.

It's all the editor of *Wisden*'s fault. Not content with devising an
unofficial world championship that placed New Zealand at the
bottom, he added insult to injury by tagging them "the world's least
charismatic team". He can't have been reading his Topsy-like
Almanack. A thousand-odd pages down the line, and still nowhere
near the end, *Wisden*'s man in Australia was heralding Stephen
Fleming's young side. Already the prototype of the team that came
to England in 1999, possessing a superb manager in John Graham
and an inspirational coach in Steve Rixon, the 1997-98 side in
Australia "included a number of gifted cricketers in their twenties
(even younger, in Daniel Vettori's case), a group epitomised by
Fleming himself, who tried to play expressive, risk-taking cricket.
They were far less nondescript than many of their predecessors and
were to leave Australia having gained in stature, popularity and a
good measure of anticipation for their next visit." Not that English
cricket writers take much notice of what's happening outside
England unless England are playing there at the time.

The bonus in being at the foot of any table is that the only way you can go is up. Except in the case of England, dumped down there by dint of losing 2-1 in the series against the uncharismatic New Zealanders. They then went to South Africa. But there's no denying that being on the bottom, even of an unofficial world championship, stung New Zealanders. The "least charismatic" jibe stuck a bit as well, but when a country has the All Blacks, the America's Cup, Sir Edmund Hillary and the brothers Finn, not to mention Bluff oysters and both varieties of Mutton Birds, you can always leave charisma to politicans, happy clappy vicars and the editor of *Wisden*.

What really tickled me about New Zealand's victory over England, apart from the two Test wins, of course, was the mantra with which the good, bad and the ugly salvaged some dross from the disaster. From the head honcho of the ECB, who must know something about cricket (if only by definition); from the *Times* cricket correspondent, who does know something; from a pensioned-off Prime Minister, who never knew much about many things; and from the Sports Minister, by Jiminy, came the balming words: "All is not lost. Only yesterday [or maybe it was the day before] England Under-19 beat the Australian Under-19s."

In other words, as Brook Benton once sang, it's all a matter of time. Or as Tom Waits observed of the Jersey girl in a see-through top as she was sipping on a soda pop, "I'll bet she's still a virgin, but it's only twenty-five to nine." All things come to those who wait.

WHEN IT COMES TO CRICKET, we New Zealanders go along with that. We went generations waiting to kick some butt – anyone's butt – because in the days before one-day cricket levelled the proverbial playing field, New Zealand were the regular rollover guys in international cricket. Mind you, being bowled out by England for 26 in 1955 was rolling-over to extremes. It didn't even help that my uncle's friend Bert Sutcliffe, whose old cut-down bat I used in our backyard games, was the only New Zealander to reach double figures: legs 11 – like my age.

We lost our virginity a year later – with the pubs closing at six o'clock you had to do something of an evening – against a West Indies side that contained Sobers, Weekes, the late, great "Collie" Smith and Ramadhin and Valentine. True, we'd lost by an innings in Dunedin and Christchurch, and by only nine wickets in Wellington. But after 26 years of Test cricket, who worried what had gone before. A schoolfriend's father, Eric Tindill, helped select the New Zealand team that won by 190 runs in Auckland, which for many men would have been their great sporting moment. Hard to say with Tindill. He'd toured Britain in 1936-37 with the All Blacks, kept wicket on New Zealand's 1937 tour of England and went on to referee international rugby and to umpire in Test cricket.

Any euphoria about New Zealand's Test standing was shortlived. It just needed a tour of diluvial England in 1958 for that. England, the Ashes Lakered and Locked away in safekeeping, were riding the crest of a wave. They won the five-Test series against New Zealand four-nil and set sail for Australia believing they were invincible. School Cert results paled into insignificance (more or less in keeping with the marks obtained) as we tuned our valve radios to long wave and hung on to Alan McGilvray's every word as Richie Benaud's resurgent Aussies elbowed (bent) England off the square. Even the testosterone took second place. It hardly mattered when May's men crossed the Tasman and lashed us by an innings in Christchurch.

We probably thought it was jolly decent of them to come. The Australians, apart from a one-Test visit after the Second World War, didn't consider us worth another Test until the Seventies. Fortunately, all this was in the days before the Australians discovered that rugby can have 15 men as well as 13, so there was a bit of sporting reciprocity. In that innings defeat by May's team, the former Australian goalkeeper, Ken Hough, amused the record crowd of 20,000 at Lancaster Park by taking 16 runs off Fred Trueman in one over. Even Fred looked amused until the number 11 thumped him back over his head for six.

More recently, New Zealand's six-hitting has been the preserve of the Cairns dynasty, if father and son are sufficient to constitute a dynasty. Father Lance put himself in the record books when he hit the country's fastest hundred, off 45 balls in 52 minutes, for Otago against Wellington in 1979-80. Of his eventual 110 runs, 98 came in boundaries (nine sixes, 11 fours). In the annals of the lusty, his hitting was up there along with Moll Flanders and Jack Nicholson.

But as Hemingway said, the son also rises, and the four sixes that Chris Cairns smote off Phil Tufnell on the Saturday of the 1999 Oval Test are already immortalised in Kiwi cricket history. Even when his 19 wickets in the series are just another line in the stats, albeit the line that set up New Zealand's victories, his life-restoring 80 from 94 balls will live among the legends. Particularly for those lucky enough to see it. Because if you were in England, weren't at the ground and hadn't gone digital, you wouldn't have seen it. While Cairns was playing the defining innings of the summer, the ECB's favoured broadcaster, Channel 4, was following the horses on its terrestrial output. So much for the ECB's promise that channel-hopping from BBC to 4 would bring a new, young audience.

CAIRNS AND CO had already enjoyed a prosperous World Cup. And why not? They were well prepared, they had a game plan and they'd recently given one of the pre-tournament favourites, South Africa, a good run for their money in a one-day series before losing 3-2. Clive Lloyd, shooting the breeze on a rainy warm-up day in Bristol, picked New Zealand as the fourth semi-finalists after Australia, Pakistan and South Africa.

People (OK, the English press) went all snooty about New Zealand's slow-medium "chokers" who took the pace off the game. But as the sweet girls say in dimestores and bus stations, there's more than one way to skin a cat. Ain't that so, Phil? It's not all pinch-hitting Sri Lankans and damp squibs in dark glasses. Sure, Chris Harris and Gavin Larsen dobbled and dobbered as is their wont, but it was the Kiwis' left-arm paceman, Geoff Allott, who took most wickets, 20, in the tournament, sharing top spot with Shane Warne. Moreover, the tick-tacking leggie snuck up on Allott only by snatching four wickets in the final.

This was the same Warne whose 10 overs went for 44 when New Zealand beat Australia in their group game at Cardiff. In terms of one-dayers between the trans-Tasman rivals, the victory went against the grain: Australia have won almost twice as many as the Kiwis. But more recently the underdogs had been twisting the Kangaroo's tail, their comeback from 2-0 down to a 2-2 drawn series in New Zealand in February 1998 being one such example.

A few months earlier, in Australia, Fleming had put his finger on his team's attitude by expressing their refusal to be "the weak little under-age side from New Zealand. We have got the ability to match it, whether verbally or aggressively, with them." At Cardiff, Roger Twose, once of Warwickshire, latterly of Wellington, and Chris Cairns mixed the ingredients in a thank you ma'am stand of 148, Cairns hitting his 60 off 77 balls and Twose finishing not out with 80 from 99. Both thumped Glenn McGrath for six and Twose dumped Warne into the River Taff to the great delight of all and sundry.

Two down (Bangladesh were easy meat first time out), three to go, the last of them Scotland – thank goodness, as it happened. At Southampton the New Zealanders came up against Walsh, Ambrose, a loose-limbed gunslinger called Dillon (why couldn't it have been the rabbit?), a white ball that seamed and swung, a coin that fell the wrong way and sun that shone after they had batted. They lost by seven wickets. At Derby their old nemesis Inzamam-ul-Haq hit them again. His 60 off 37 balls had stopped New Zealand in the semi-finals of the 1991-92 World Cup; now he made nonsense of a slow pitch by hitting seven fours in his unbeaten 73. Ijaz Ahmed couldn't manage one in his 51. As for the slow pitch, Shoaib Akhtar made as much a nonsense of that as he did of New Zealand's opening pair, caught behind for one and none disrespectfully. Happily, seeing things in a wider context, Fleming (69) and Harris (42) put on 83 for the seventh wicket. It didn't save New Zealand from defeat by 62 runs, but with Australia and West Indies playing silly buggers at Old Trafford, net run-rates were all important when the Kiwis went to Edinburgh. By despatching Scotland cheaply and passing their total quickly, they stayed in the World Cup and West Indies went home.

Leeds did the dirty on New Zealand in their first Super Six game, ending day one early and washing out the reserve day altogether when they looked to have Zimbabwe for the taking. Allott and Cairns were the prime lambs that day, Cairns the slaughtered one four days later when the Kiwis came up against the more southern African nation. Hansie Cronje heaved him for two sixes and Jacques Kallis for one in an over costing 24 runs as South Africa ran up an unbeatable 287 for five. At least Allott had the consolation of becoming the top wicket-taker in any World Cup when he bowled

Herschelle Gibbs for 91. Some bright spark noticed that the previous record-holders, Roger Binny (1983), Craig McDermott (1987) and Wasim Akram (1992) had been World Cup winners. Allott, sad to say, broke the mould.

A nail-biting victory over India, the nerves not helped by a thunderstorm that halted play with New Zealand still needing 58 from 58 balls, saw them into another semi-final against Pakistan. Again it was a fence too far. Shoaib, the Rawalpindi Express, shunted them into a siding every time they threatened to get beyond their station, searing yorkers sending back Nathan Astle, Fleming and Harris – not forgetting their stumps. On another day a total of 241 for seven might have been defendable, but it needed early wickets. The first came when Pakistan were 194, a World Cup record for the first wicket, and it was the only one to fall.

WHEN THE OTHER countries went home to show off their silverware, lick their wounds or polish their tarnished pride (the English were already back in the comfort zone they call county cricket), the New Zealanders settled into the second part of a campaign that had been 18 months in preparation. In truth it began before that with the appointment in 1996 of Rixon, the former New South Wales and Australia wicketkeeper. Chosen ahead of 16 other applicants to replace the displaced Glenn Turner as coach, "Stumper" Rixon had coached New South Wales to three Sheffield Shield titles and came with the requisite man-management skills for a team in turmoil. Cairns and Adam Parore, for example, were not offered contracts for 1996-97, when England toured, because of breaches of New Zealand Cricket's code of conduct. Both had been critical of Turner's leadership. Their performances in England were adequate testimony to the way they responded to Rixon.

Complementing Rixon's methods was the quiet authority of the manager, John Graham. Until recently headmaster of Auckland Boys' Grammar School, "DJ" brought to his job the kind of credentials only a select few in New Zealand could match. He'd been an All Black, a flanker in the glory days of Wilson Whinerary at the back end of the Fifties and front end of the Sixties. In a country of iconoclasts, men who've worn the Black jersey are the closest thing to icons. Most New Zealanders wouldn't raise their face from the Axminster in the presence of one. Appointing a former All Black to manage New Zealand's cricketers was as good as guaranteeing that they'd walk on water for him, a useful attribute for a team coming to England in May and staying until August.

The final piece in the management jigsaw was Fleming's appointment. New Zealand's youngest captain at 23 when he stood in for Lee Germon in the final Test against Mike Atherton's tourists in 1997, he impressed Rixon from the start as "a strong human being internally. You see a guy who keeps good strong emotions in his face throughout the game and looks like he's in full control out there. He's perceived as a guy who's very cool on the ground and he understands the team requirement versus the individual requirement."

Added to which he was naturally gracious, was his country's most talented batsman, had few peers as a slip catcher and possessed a useful, self-deprecating sense of humour. Asked after the 1997-98 tour of Australia if his team needed fine-tuning, Fleming replied: "Fine-tuning! We haven't got anything to fine tune, we're still looking for a station and all we're getting is static."

"That tour of Australia was one of the areas we had to go through to become the side we're starting to become now," reckoned Rixon after New Zealand's maiden Test win at Lord's. "It was a hard and bitter pill to swallow but it was one we could only have learnt from and I think the guys have taken a lot of the hardness of the Australians, the way they play their state cricket, and their general hardness in attitude."

What that tour also proved was that New Zealand were on the right wavelength by bringing on youngsters at the expense of older, still-established players such as Danny Morrison, Mark Greatbatch and Bryan Young. Of the Under-19 team that won its "Test" series in England in 1996, Vettori graduated to the Test team several months later, against England, after just two first-class games; Craig McMillan, the captain, went to Australia where he reached his maiden Test fifty with a six off Warne (his first Test hundred came three months later with a six off Zimbabwe's leg-spinning Adam Huckle); and Matthew Bell built on hitting the winning runs at Lord's

Appointing a

All Black

New Zealand's

as good as guar

they'd walk on

a useful **attr**

coming to Eng

staying until

former

to manage

cricketers was

anteeing that

water for him,

pute for a team

and in May and

August

by underpinning the New Zealand innings at Old Trafford with a disciplined 83 off 224 balls (well, it was a Test). The only winners at Manchester, though, were the weather, and Kelly and Cherie Winter of Christchurch. Slim, blonde and pretty, a frequent attraction for the television cameras at Lord's, the Winter sisters have romantic claims on the Old Trafford ton-up twins, Astle (101) and McMillan (107 not out).

Gerald Howat, reviewing that 1996 Under-19 tour for *Wisden*, could not have been more on the button when he wrote: "The adult New Zealand Test team has been going through a lean patch, but this might not go on for too long." I nurtured similar hopes in 1989 when I watched a New Zealand Under-19 team containing Cairns, Parore and Harris win their "Test" series against a Young England team replete with future Test cricketers in Mark Ramprakash, Nick Knight, John Crawley, Dominic Cork, Darren Gough, Mark Ilott and Ian Salisbury. Harris scored a hundred and Cairns, bowling fast and straight, took 10 wickets when New Zealand won by an innings at Scarborough. Maybe it was optimistic to think that New Zealand had a star in the wings for when Richard Hadlee called it a day, but as it happened they did. It's just that it took the best part of a decade for Cairns to come to terms with his undoubted talent.

That decade began on a note of celebration for New Zealand with Test wins against India and Australia in early 1990. The 10-wicket victory over India in Christchurch saw Hadlee take his 400th Test wicket; at Wellington he hit his 3,000th Test run as the Aussies were beaten by nine wickets. After that Indian summer, however, it was downhill all the way in the Test world. In their 59 Tests throughout the Eighties, New Zealand had won 17 (29%) and lost 15 (25%), their best return ever (by way of instructive comparison, the same period saw England play 104 Tests, winning 20 [19%] and losing 39 [37%]). In 55 Tests from 1990 until Fleming's appointment as official captain, against Sri Lanka in March 1997, the sorry record was just seven wins (12%) against 25 defeats (45%). (England's record, in 77 Tests, was won 19 [24%] and lost 29 [37%].)

Perhaps it's not surprising that New Zealand cricket embraced a 10-overs-a-side slog called Cricket Max in an attempt to sustain some public interest. It had been devised as midsummer Sunday entertainment by Crowe and Sky Television, but it was midsummer madness having players going straight from Cricket Max into Test cricket. "I don't think an enormous amount of thought went into the programme," said new coach Rixon with a surprising degree of understatement for an Australian.

New Zealand's decline is not difficult to pinpoint. Their success in the Eighties was built around a nucleus of experienced players in Geoff Howarth, Hadlee, John Wright and Martin Crowe, who honed their skills in county cricket, just as Turner had before them. But new restrictions on overseas players closed the door of this particular academy to the next generation. When Hadlee and then Wright retired in the early Nineties, Crowe was the lone star in a state of flux. He marshalled New Zealand to the World Cup semi-finals in 1992, but Test triumphs (two wins against seven defeats in 16 games as captain) proved as elusive as status and sympathy in the land of the long white cloud.

New Zealand's leading run-scorer in international cricket, Crowe perceived himself as a victim of "tall poppy syndrome" at home. Maybe, maybe not. It could be that the only tall poppies cultivated in New Zealand have all-black petals. And as Olympic 800 and 1500 metres champion Peter Snell found to his cost, his countrymen have an innate facility for the none-too-subtle put-down: "You've won three gold medals, eh. So what do you in life, Pete?" In the end Snell, ranked Athlete of the Sixties by America's *Track and Field News* magazine, packed his bags and went to live in California. When you return to New Zealand, said Jane Campion, director of the 1993 Palme d'Or winning film, *The Piano*, "the first thing you put in the suitcase is your humility". In other words, forget the fact that many people in England think you're one of the most elegant, classical batsmen of your era. You're just another Kiwi.

HOWEVER, IT'S easy to forget that it took Hadlee time to savour victory over England. First capped at 20 (Cairns played his first Test at 19), Hadlee was 26 when his 10 wickets at Wellington in February 1978 saw New Zealand home against England for the first time. And 32 when New Zealand won their first Test on English soil at the 29th attempt. He didn't take a wicket in that game at Leeds in 1983

The New Ball

but conceded fewer than two runs an over from 47 overs and scored 75 in the first innings. Lance Cairns, closing on 34, took the bowling honours with 10 wickets, including the first haul of seven in an innings against England by a New Zealander. It was a different story, however, when the Kiwis won again in 1986. On home ground at Trent Bridge, 35-year-old Hadlee took 10 wickets and scored 68 runs in the eight-wicket victory that also gave them their first series win in England.

I wasn't on the ground the day of those victories, which is why I knew I shouldn't have been at Edgbaston the Saturday of the first Test of 1999. True, the pundits were predicting a New Zealand win, but my bones said different. England, with nine wickets in hand, needed another 204 for victory. In their first innings, they had managed only 126, while New Zealand's second-innings 107 on the second afternoon was taken to show the fallibility of the pitch as much as New Zealand's batting. The problem for the Kiwis was that the sun shone on Saturday morning, and they came out knowing that their batting had blown it on Friday. You could see it in their body language and in the way they bowled. All credit to young Alex Tudor for the way he attacked the bowling, taking the game away with his 99 not out. But Fleming knew the truth: "We threw it away in one session of cricket and that hurt us. It hurt me." The pain was there to see behind his eyes.

That defeat hurt me as well, which is why I wasn't present when the coup de grâce was delivered at Lord's and The Oval. I remember writing, though, that Lord's could be the time "for Cairns to stand up and be counted as a Test cricketer. His country needs him." It needed him even more when opening bowler Simon Doull, so impressive in England's first innings at Edgbaston, twisted his knee against Hampshire and had to have surgery. Cairns knew his time had come, too. At Canterbury, on a pitch on which New Zealand ground out 591, their highest total in England, he took seven wickets as Kent were bowled out for 201 in their first innings. Come the Lord's Test, he weighed in with six for 77 when England crashed to 186 all out in their first innings. He bowled fast, he bowled slow(ish) and as someone who'd taken his share of stick from Australian sledgers in the past, he took no lip.

122

"You're in the big boys' game now," said Graham Thorpe unwisely after hitting him for four. "Who's playing with the big boys now?" yelled a jubilant Cairns when he bowled Thorpe with his beautifully-concealed slower ball at Lord's. It was his second success over Thorpe in the game. Much was made of Cairns' slower ball, especially when poor Chris Read ducked under it, thinking he was getting a beamer, and was more or less yorked. But I recall Nottinghamshire's Franklyn Stephenson doing something similar to the Essex opener, Brian Hardie, in the 1989 Benson and Hedges Cup final, and as a youngster Cairns was a Trent Bridge team-mate of Stephenson for a time. The time wasn't wasted.

Matt Horne's six-hour century on the second day consolidated New Zealand's position at Lord's and Vettori set them up for a sunny Saturday with as uncomplicated a half-century as you could wish to see – until you saw the reprise at The Oval in the final Test, when it was even more valuable. On both occasions, the left-arm spinner – he also bats left-handed – gave himself room to drive and carve through the off side, and as often as not the England bowlers obliged by putting the ball where he liked hitting it. No-one ever expected England's left-arm spinner, Phil Tufnell, to match Vettori's batting, but few expected that the 20-year-old veteran of 23 Tests would outbowl the Middlesex man in the series. By The Oval he was in a groove all of his own, reeling his way through 33 overs in England's first innings (three for 46) and introducing a dipping arm ball as deadly and delightful as Cairns' slower delivery.

Floppy-haired, bespectacled, grinning like the schoolboy he'd just stopped being when he was dropped into Test cricket, Vettori summed up everything about Fleming's New Zealanders. They were young, quick to learn and articulate; they played with attitude and a smile. They'd done some hard travelling together, and if England was anything to go by, the road was just beginning. ☽

No FLAGGING INDIAN SUPPORTER, EDGBASTON

FLY AWAY PAUL, COME BACK PETER A RUEFUL REIFFEL AFTER HIS
THROW HAD KILLED A PIGEON, THE OVAL

Keith Booth

The Number-Muncher's Tale

Keith Booth, a Yorkshireman
and former university administrator,
is now well established in his second
career of scoring and writing.
He has completed six seasons with
Surrey, having previously worked
with Middlesex, MCC and the
Test Match Special team, and has
covered over a dozen Tests and
about twice that number of one-day
internationals. His second book
Knowing the Score is just on the
market and his third, a biography of
Surrey's infamous 19th-century
wicketkeeper, Edward Pooley, is
seeking a publisher.

Wickedest wicket From an
18th-century scoresheet - "Run out
– Lord Tankerville's fault".

Soundest bite PA announcer
at Derby during Pakistan-New
Zealand World Cup match:
"Please keep off the outfield during
play ... Will spectators please keep
off the pitch. Please respect ... Oh,
I give up."

"The coach will leave at 10.30 am for Loch Ness". The message flashed on the television screens in the rooms of the Pakistan team was clear enough, and indicated that the Spanish receptionist at the £250-plus per night Royal Garden Hotel in Kensington had a tolerable awareness of UK tourist spots but, despite the hotel billing itself as the "Headquarters of the World Cup", an ignorance of all things cricketing. For "Loch Ness" read "Lord's Nets" and the notice began to make some kind of sense.

It was symptomatic of a month and a half of behind-the-scenes disorganisation that left me foundering between the Scylla of the World Cup organising committee and the Charybdis of the Pakistan Cricket Board and trying to avoid sundry minor rocks and whirlpools in between like Old Trafford gatemen, Headingley dressing-room attendants and Rushmans, the media accreditation agency.

It completed a happy day. What on grounds other than Lord's had been a 10-minute job of collecting complimentary tickets and checking the scoring facility took about four hours, not far off the actual playing time in the final. The obvious place to collect World Cup tickets seemed to be the World Cup Office. No comps for players and officials were available from the MCC office, which saw no reason (it was, after all, only Lord's, only a World Cup final) to vary its normal opening hours of 1pm to 3pm. Fine. Wait for the place to open and collect the tickets. Unfortunately, the hospitality tickets which accompany the entrance tickets were available from the World

Cup Office, where the girl who dealt with them had gone to lunch. No, there was no one else who could deal with it.

So there was plenty of time while waiting for the MCC office to open to check the scorebox, adjacent to the old press box in the Warner Stand. If the power points or telephone lines were not working, then it would be useful to find out now rather than half an hour before the start of the match. Except the aged and half-witted flunkey on the Grace Gates seemed totally incapable of understanding the words "the scorebox adjacent to the old press box in the Warner Stand" and took three attempts to find the key. At the beginning of attempt three, the Australian team arrived. I was greeted by my former Surrey colleague Brendon Julian.

"G'day, Boothy: you scoring the final?"

"Only if the scorebox key can be located: otherwise it won't get done!"

THE ORGANISATION of the 1999 World Cup reminded me somewhat of Samuel Johnson's comment on Milton, that he could cut a colossus out of a rock but could not carve heads upon cherry-stones. With the odd exception the format of the tournament, the hotel and transport arrangements all worked well, but minor details such as the welfare of match officials received attention that was at best cursory and at worst non-existent.

Umpires and match referees were briefed at Lord's a couple of days before the first warm-up matches. They were given: 1) a set of playing conditions amended orally at the 11th hour to bring runs scored from wides into line with standard practice for limited-overs internationals (had I not had breakfast with Doug Cowie, the New Zealand umpire, a couple of days later, I would never have known and my colleagues somehow picked it up by osmosis); 2) a couple of shirts; 3) a couple of maps. They were then decanted on to St John's Wood Road to find their way to their first assignments – by public transport. All had luggage with them to last seven weeks. Some knew the UK pretty well; for others, it was their first visit and they had scant knowledge of transport networks.

Sailab Hossain, Bangladesh's representative on the umpires panel, was allegedly overheard asking passers-by for directions to the London Railway Station. As he managed to show up for his first commitment in Durham, it has to be asssumed that some kind soul informed him that there were a dozen or so railway terminuses in London and that the one he wanted was Kings Cross. Steve Bucknor, his colleague for the Scotland-Durham warm-up match, was spotted by the Scotland team at a bus stop in Durham City. He was welcomed on board the coach and transported to the Riverside Ground in Chester-le-Street. Had the tournament underdogs been less observant, he would have been dependent on the local bus service – and who knows how frequent or reliable that might be. Here was a man good enough to umpire a World Cup final, but not considered important enough to be provided with transport to get him round the country.

The umpires and match referees were a pretty resilient, streetwise bunch because most of them happened to be rather illustrious, well-travelled types such as Peter Burge, Darrell Hair and John Reid. Some equipped themselves with hire cars for the duration of the tournament, but when competing teams were rightly provided with a luxury coach, car and luggage van, their treatment seems shabby in the extreme. To have provided them with transport would not have made too many deep inroads into the finances of a tournament which turned over some £50m.

Still, at least umpires and match officials were paid – or I assume they were (the organisation – I use the word loosely – below the tip of the iceberg meant it was impossible to be certain of anything). Scorers were not. True, the hotel accommodation was certainly of high quality and the daily allowance of £45 sufficient to cover a couple of decent meals, laundry etc. However, although letters of appointment did not spell it out, most had taken it as understood out that the usual ECB fee, complimentary ticket and hospitality package would apply. It came as something of a shock when we discovered at the briefing meeting in January that this was not intended to be the case.

There would be no pay and any complimentary tickets would have to come from the team's allocation of 75 per match. And with a resident Pakistani population of a million or so in the UK, most claiming to be cousins, uncles, nephews and nieces of Wasim Akram, there was fat chance of that. To be fair, the ECB relented on that one and provided a couple of complimentary tickets and hospitality packages for each match; they were also generous with medals, end-of-tournament parties, shirts, letters of thanks, but kind words butter no parsnips. Scorers whose teams were eliminated at the group stage were invited to score for the press at £100 per day plus expenses. Those whose teams were unfortunate enough to be left in continued to receive expenses only. The longer they stayed in, the further out-of-pocket were their scorers.

My arrangement with Surrey was that they would continue to pay my salary, but deduct a day's pay for each match day I missed. It is highly ironic, however, that 12 months after changing its rules to avoid the possibility of being considered a trade union, the Association of County Cricket Scorers should adopt one of trade unionism's most restrictive practices, namely the pre-entry closed shop: candidacy for World Cup scoring appointments was restricted to ACCS members. Having thus narrowed the field, however, the association was in no position to help its members secure decent contracts. So while the England players were negotiating a deal that would have brought them £60,000 and the sight of bacon in the trees had they won the World Cup, scorers meekly accepted legally dubious contracts that provided a rate of £3.60 below the recently-introduced national minimum wage. On the other hand, this corresponded to the match fee received by the amateurs of Scotland. A slow over-rate against Pakistan resulted in coach Jim Love announcing to the dressing room: "Lads, the bad news is that we've been fined: the good news is that the fine is 5% of fuck all."

THE TREATMENT OF SCORERS during the World Cup was entirely consistent with the practice of the last couple of hundred years (see Chapter 6 of my book *Knowing the Score* on the Status and Pay of Scorers if you've nothing better to do). At Headingley, where I reported for duty for the Australia–Pakistan Group B match, not only their status and pay, but even their existence was called into question.

I had not come across Rushmans Accreditation Services before, except insofar as they had provided me – late – with an "All Venues" piece of plastic to get me into grounds, and I had read in the minutes of the Cricket Writers' Club AGM of its members' "concern and anger" and unanimous vote of no-confidence in the capability of said organisation to do its job properly. If their earlier administration had been anything like that which obtained in the Headingley press box, then "concern and anger" was an incredibly mild reaction.

Part of said press box is also used as the scorers' "box", hardly ideal at the best of times but tolerable in county matches when the place is not too full and it's warm and dry and behind the bowler's arm. Conversely, the disadvantages are that no sound penetrates there from the outer world, so that there is no atmosphere. It is like watching television with the sound turned down. The requirement under the Laws for the umpires to call and signal to the scorers is hence rendered purely academic. While a call of "No Ball", "Wide Ball", "One Short", whatever, may be perfectly audible to the 18,000 or so people in the ground – and, at this particular match, on the roofs of the adjacent terraced houses – it falls on deafened ears in the scoring area. Furthermore, because of the darkened glass, covered in black netting for matches involving coloured clothing and white balls, the umpires cannot see the scorers' acknowledgement of their signals. So the scorers can't hear the umpires and the umpires can't hear the scorers. Apart from that, it's OK.

All this pales into insignificance, mind, when there is no scoring position at all. Which was the situation in which Australia's scorer, Darrin White and I found ourselves on the morning of Sunday May 23. Scorers will arrive at any club or village ground and there will be a scoring position: it may be a shed, shared with redundant ground equipment and a colony of spiders, it may be an al fresco rickety chair and disused kitchen table, but at least there is one. On a Test ground, staging a key World Cup fixture, there wasn't. Every seat was allocated to the press, those normally reserved for the scorers – where there is a direct telephone link to enable their laptops to be linked to the Press Association – being occupied by the representative of the *Karachi Chronicle*.

My request to the Rushmans representatives as to where it was intended to locate the scorers was met with "You should have an orange sticker" followed by a display of ignorance normally reserved for inebriated committee members as they try to unravel the difference between scorers and scoreboard operators. A steward at The Oval once responded to a request to speak to someone higher up by standing on an orange box. No orange box was available here, but it took the eventual intervention of the ECB's technical director and the Yorkshire chief executive to ensure that a club with a long and distinguished pedigree did not become a cosmic laughing-stock through depriving some 150m or so internet subscribers of their fix of World Cup cricket.

The bedside lamp which, with East Riding ingenuity, John Potter, the Yorkshire scorer, had acquired from his local B&Q to acknowledge the umpires' signals, was nowhere to be found, so I warned Peter Willey and Rudi Koertzen that unless it was, their signals would remain unacknowledged. "So, what's new?" retorted Willey. Miraculously and mysteriously, it did eventually emerge from somewhere.

Even then space was limited. Scorers these days need a bit of room for laptops and printers, reference books and two or three clipboards. Once the *sine qua non* of laptop and printer were installed there was space for half a clipboard. So I kept a linear sheet only: the scorecard proper and bowling analysis were completed next day.

I can honestly say that these were the worst scoring conditions I have experienced, not excluding those at The Oval on bread-and-circus days when cricket took second place to second-rate marketing and the scorebox was shared unequally with the DJ responsible for the music accompanying players to the wicket and inept and inane comments on the state of play.

The Headingley drama was all on top of the team coach being denied access to the ground because it had arrived at 8.55, five minutes before the gates were due to open. And Pakistan's captain, who has been around for a while and is tolerably well known on the county circuit, being denied access to the dressing room on the grounds that he hadn't brought his pass. Wasim's way round this administrative dilemma was beautifully simple. He ignored the directive and walked straight in. It was something of a relief that Pakistan qualified from Group B in first place and a Super Six route of Trent Bridge, Old Trafford and The Oval, thus leaving the scorers of New Zealand, Zimbabwe, Australia (again) and South Africa to benefit from the Headingley experience.

EVEN THOUGH, AS A YORKSHIREMAN, it grieves me to say so, the scoring position at Old Trafford is everything that Headingley is not – spacious, quiet and, while adjacent to the press, separated from them by the ingenious device of a wall and a door. Its main disadvantage is that it's a long walk from the dining room and when there are books to balance and innings and Duckworth/Lewis print-outs to do, 45 minutes is just insufficient to do it all, walk to lunch, have lunch and get back again in time for the second session; to say nothing of the physical impossibility of getting through a capacity crowd such as that present for the India-Pakistan Super Six match. Fortunately, we were able to sneak (with permission) a couple of the lunch boxes provided for the press.

Quite acceptable, and Plan B for the semi-final a week later against New Zealand. Plan A was for a steward to escort us across the outfield to the dining room, but that was to be abandoned if the first session ran beyond 2.15 and reduced the interval to less than 45 minutes. It did. I had briefed the Rushmans people about our requirements and while scorers were not their responsibility (the scorers were no one's responsibility) they were quite happy to help if they could and would let us know in good time if they couldn't, so that alternative arrangements might be made. "In good time" turned out to be after 49.3 overs – ie slap-bang in the middle of the end-of-innings flurry.

The last over of a one-day innings is normally one which requires 110% concentration from the scorers. Dot balls are a rare as snowballs in the Sahara and there is usually a cascade of runs or wickets – often both – with scrambled leg-byes, run outs and batsmen crossing on catches. The news of a lunchtime fast took a while to sink in. A hastily concocted Plan C (sending off the reserve scorer to find a hot dog and coffee stall) at least ensured a minimum level of nourishment to sustain us through the second innings.

The letter from the ACCS secretary inviting applications for World Cup scoring appointments notified an intention to appoint upgraded "Match Managers" to deal, inter alia, with any problems caused by scorers' unfamiliarity with venues which, with rare exceptions, were on grounds other than their own. Umpires were underpinned throughout by a fourth official and in the latter stages the match referees had the support of a reserve, but the only "Match Managers" of any kind we saw were the Duckworth/Lewis ones (including Duckworth and Lewis themselves) and their expertise was not required at any stage of the tournament; the upgraded ones we hadn't seen yet.

So it was self-help throughout (but scorers are used to that). Never more so than during the India-Pakistan match at Old Trafford when my colleague John Blondel, scoring for India, was taken ill midway through the Pakistan innings. Fortunately, Alan West, Lancashire's regular scorer, was with us, scoring the match for the Old Trafford international scorebook, and through his familiarity with the ground's internal administration was able to summon help from the St John's Ambulance people fairly rapidly while I carried on recording the match.

The last thing John remembered doing before losing consciousness was recording Moin Khan's dismissal, caught by Tendulkar at long leg. While the world continued without him, Abdur Razzaq – voted Man of the Tournament by the British Scrabble Association – came in, pulled a calf muscle hitting a six and Moin returned as his runner. Meantime, poor old John had responded to the attentions of the paramedics and his first glimpse of reality was Moin, at the non-striker's end, squad number and name clearly displayed. So John drew the inevitable conclusion – he had put the wrong batsman out – and promptly passed out again. In retrospect, it was amusing. It might have been anything but.

QUITE FRANKLY, scoring services were provided on the cheap. The financial arrangements which would have left most 1st XI scorers out of pocket meant that the responsibility was entrusted largely to 2nd XI scorers. Willing and conscientious though they were, they lacked international experience, they lacked computer experience, they lacked experience of dealing with the media and they lacked experience of Duckworth/Lewis. The target in one of

One Pakistan player said: "Pakistanis are **lovely** people, great cricketers, but **shit** organisers" the warm-up matches was cocked up: it didn't matter. It was a friendly match; the margin of victory was large. It might have mattered. It might have been a closer match in the final stages of the competition with a six-figure sum riding on the result.

The scoring itself was quite pressurised. Much as one tried to persuade oneself that each match was just another game, the public interest and media pressure were such that it was pretty important to have the score right and up-to-date all the time. Perhaps my proudest achievement was to reproduce, error-free on laptop and scoresheet, Saqlain Mushtaq's first over against Bangladesh. It began with a wide, one run, another wide, a leg-bye then five wides (laptop crosses batsmen on odd number of runs: cross them back again because its a wide which has gone to the boundary and they stay where they are). After another single, Mehrab Hossein was stumped off a wide, whereupon Akram Khan, bless him, played three dot balls. Six legal deliveries, four illegal ones, 10 from the over (eight wides and two singles), Saqlain 1-0-10-1 and with the leg-bye, 11 on the total. I'm pleased there weren't too many like that.

Mind you, the Scotland-Pakistan match at times came pretty close: when Pakistan's score stood at 92 for five, 45 had come in extras. It slowed down after that and ended up at 59, a World Cup record, equalling the record for all limited-overs internationals. Umpires Cowie and Ian Robinson indicated at the interval that had we been able to let them know (through the third umpire) that they were so close, they would certainly have gone for it.

Lest the reader should think that scoring was the only area to which the cock-up theory applied, let me relate just one anecdote of multiple maladministration. It was not the only one by any means, but the editor of *The New Ball* is not blessed with unlimited space. It was one of those occasions where everybody thought everyone else was to blame but no one involved was prepared to take the responsibility. The brewery, certainly, would have been left without the proverbial piss-up.

There were three clear days for the Pakistan team to get from Bristol, where they had beaten West Indies on the first Sunday, to Durham where they were to play Scotland the following Thursday. It is possible to travel most of the way from Bristol to Durham by motorway and the team had a luxury coach at their disposal. However, the organisers came to the conclusion that the obvious way of transporting the squad from the south-west to the north-east was by Tuesday's 7.45am flight from Bristol to Newcastle, which meant a 5am wake-up call or, as some journalists would have us believe, an earlier-than-usual departure from the city-centre nightclubs. The coach would take them to the airport for a 7am check-in and meet them in Newcastle after a leisurely 200 mph cruise along the M5, M42 and M1. For a moment, sanity prevailed. Another coach would meet them at the airport and duly arrived in good time – at Teesside Airport 50 miles from where the BA flight would land.

No problem. A third bus was arranged to meet the team at the right airport. So now we have three buses heading towards Newcastle, one on the M5 between Bristol and Birmingham, one on the A1(M) between Middlesbrough and Newcastle and one between Newcastle city centre and the airport. None actually arrive in time: so streaming in the other direction towards the Royal County Hotel in Durham is a fleet of taxis commandeered by the squad who have meantime landed and found no transport to meet them. They duly arrive at their destination to find that, as it is still mid-morning and check-out time being noon, their rooms are still occupied by the previous night's guests. Meanwhile, the team liaison officer, having organised the whole operation from a traffic jam in Bristol city centre, has turned the wrong way on to the M4 and is heading towards South Wales. Who pays how much for what, is, I believe, still being sorted out.

Of course, being attached to Wasim and company meant regular reminders of their supporters' unbounded passion. The mood of the Old Trafford gateman matched the weather as I announced myself as the Pakistan scorer. "You're the third one we've had this morning," he said grimly, an indication of the enthusiasm and the lengths to which the the local and visiting Pakistani community would go to gain entry to grounds staging World Cup fixtures. And that was for a warm-up match against Lancashire that Manchester's monsoons allowed very little chance of being played. In the later stages of the competition, those who were unable to gain entry resourcefully found themselves a convenient vantage point on any neighbouring tall building overlooking the ground.

Polite requests over the public address system in English and Urdu, in the name of the captain, for the playing area not be encroached on during play and for the dignity of the players to be respected were about as much use as a chocolate teapot. It was an eye-opener to those who associate cricket with rural calm, deckchairs and cream teas and incredibly refreshing to see the kind of enthusiasm and support which has been absent from English grounds for the last generation. As a scorer, I normally record the times of and reasons for stoppages: usually it is something like 5.10-5.35 Bad Light; 12.05-1.15 Rain (Early lunch), 2.10-2.13 Injury to Bloggs. "4.44-4.47 Firecrackers, 6.12-6.20 Pitch invasion" are ones I don't expect to have to repeat too often.

AND NOW THE TUMULT and shouting have died and the captains and the kings departed (I associate myself with the *Financial Times*, the only national newspaper not to use the cliche, "The Carnival is Over") and several hundred thousand words expended on the quality of the leading exponents of limited-overs cricket compared with the lack of quality of the host nation. I have no wish to add to that except to say that it might not be unconnected to a more statistical and scientific approach. The kind long used by Bob Woolmer in his coaching of the South African team and adopted by other coaches, notably Richard Pybus of Border who impressed the Pakistanis on their early 1998 tour of the Republic and was invited to join them as assistant coach for the World Cup.

No one would claim that statistics alone can win cricket matches, but statistics sensibly applied (as opposed to statistics produced in the interest of statisticians) can produce useful and applicable information on the strengths and weaknesses of one's own team and of the opposition. "Boothy," said one of the Pakistan players to me, "Pakistanis are lovely people, great cricketers, but shit organisers." That recognised, the natural talent of the players and allowing others to do the organising for them proved an effective combination – until the final.

If the nature and quality of its scorebook is a barometer of a nation's organisational capacity, then the observation is absolutely spot-on. Pakistan didn't have one. From time to time, some scorer, such as Darnley Boxill in Barbados, will propose a standardised scoresheet for use worldwide in limited-overs internationals. To an extent that was achieved in the World Cup through the identical software installed on the laptops, but the pencil-and-paper systems varied enormously. South Africa had a special gold-embossed scorebook, New Zealand a Dickensian-type ledger too large to fit into any known scorebox (except possibly the Headingley press box on a quiet day), West Indies a dog-eared paperback which resembled an overgrown school exercise book. Bangladesh bought a standard Bourne book when they got here. Pakistan's deeds were recorded on purloined Surrey scoresheets and mailed *ex post facto* to the Pakistan Cricket Board.

A detailed study of the correlation between scoresheets and approaches to cricket is not part of my brief here, but Pakistan would in any case buck such an exercise by having a coach whose analytical approach complemented the natural flair on which they rely. The scorers' laptops can produce "starbursts" which indicate where a batsman is scoring runs or where a bowler is conceding them. They can be used in match preparation albeit with the obvious caveat that they indicate only where the ball has gone, not how it got there. So a line at 45 degrees behind the wicket could indicate a late cut or an involuntary thick edge while a chart which indicated that a batsman's strengths are square of the wicket, as Graham Thorpe's usually does, would encourage bowlers to adjust their line and length accordingly. It is an approach that is now almost second nature to coaches in South Africa, Australia and New Zealand and one that Duncan Fletcher has used with Western Province and South Africa A. It will have something of a novelty value if he applies it to England.

After each match I produced such starbursts, as well as the usual scorecards and averages plus competition strike rates of opposing batsmen and teams and par 50-over scores for the next ground. Early in the Super Six stages, after Pakistan in the wake of their defeat by Bangladesh had lost to India and South Africa, it became increasingly apparent that, as had happened at the group stage, net run-rate could have a role to play in determining the final placings. The likelihood was that, in the last round of matches, the teams for which the games had more significance would have the higher motivation, that New Zealand would beat India (who could not qualify for the semi-final) and Australia would beat South Africa (who had already qualified). It was therefore important for Pakistan to beat Zimbabwe by the largest margin of runs possible to up their run-rate and qualify for the semi-finals in first place, thereby avoiding South Africa and Australia who would thus finish second and third.

And so it transpired. Pakistan were a little fortunate in that other results went their way, but at least they considered the consequences of net run-rate in time to do something about it. So did Australia when perversely they deliberately slowed down their scoring rate in an ultimately vain attempt to take West Indies through to the Super Sixes with them at the expense of New Zealand. Conversely, England, having failed to up their run rate against Zimbabwe and Kenya, only began to think about it when Zimbabwe reduced South Africa to 40 for six. The impression created was all too plain: too much "Up, boys and at 'em" and too little reasoned planning. Much, much too late did England read the rules. Like the Presbyterian tale of the sinners before the Lord, "We didna ken, we didna ken" was the cry. And the Lord replied, "Ye ken the noo".

THIS ARTICLE could not be complete without some reference to the allegations of impropriety among the Pakistan team and riotous living the night before the final. It doesn't make for good copy and it is not possible to prove a negative, but all I can say is that I was not aware of any. Nor am I able to say anything about allegations of match-fixing. There were certainly no references to it in my hearing and, not being party to the Qayyum Report, I cannot comment with any authority on what might have gone on over the last four years. However, I have no reason to doubt the sincerity and validity of the captain's statement that Pakistan is a gambling nation and when things go wrong and a scapegoat is required the team gets the blame. Sport and politics are inseparable. In Pakistan, there are no half measures, no golden mean. It is a short swing of the pendulum from national heroes for getting to the final to national villains for losing it.

There had been nightclubbing and dancing earlier in the

tournament, especially after the semi-final win against New Zealand at Old Trafford, but very little drinking. Most of the team are devout Muslims and consequently teetotal. The night before the final (so far as I am aware) consisted of a non-alcoholic team meal at a Lebanese restaurant on the Edgware Road and an early night for this young, disciplined side – and for their less young and less disciplined scorer, unsuccessfully trying to persuade himself that this was just another fixture, but acutely aware that it was almost certainly the biggest one-day match he would ever do.

At the end of the day, despite the hassle, despite the financial arrangements, despite the disppointment of the final, it was an experience on which most of the scorers will look back with nostalgia and affection. The opportunity to spend seven weeks with the world's leading players, coaches and officials – to say nothing of a royal reception at Buckingham Palace – is not one which occurs too often. The next World Cup in England will not be until well into the next millennium, by which time some of us may have swapped our scoreboxes for caskets.

PAKISTAN GONNA WIN-
FIRST THE
WORLD CUP
THEN
KASHMIR!

KASHMIR IF YOU CAN PAKISTAN SUPPORTER STRESSES THE PRIORITIES DURING HOSTILITIES V INDIA, OLD TRAFFORD

WHEN THE HEAT HITS THE FAN AUSTRALIA v ZIMBABWE, LORD'S

Stephen Bates

Legless In Amstelveen

Stephen Bates has played cricket (and occasionally worked for) the *Reading Chronicle*, *Oxford Mail*, BBC at Pebble Mill, the *Daily Telegraph*, *Daily Mail* and the *Guardian*. He currently combines being fixtures secretary of the Royal Brussels Cricket Club and European Affairs Editor of the *Guardian*.

Wickedest wicket John Inverarity, lbw b Underwood 56, 27 August 1968, The Oval, allowing England to square the Ashes series via a 226-run victory with six minutes to spare. It was the first Test I ever saw, a 14 year-old mad with excitement.

Soundest bite "I don't expect to get a wicket. Here's Hollies. Bradman pushes the ball gently in the direction of the Houses of Parliament. It doesn't go that far of course – it merely goes to Watkins at silly mid-off ... Hollies pitches the ball up, slowly ... and he's bowled. (Pause) Bradman, bowled Hollies, nought. And what do you say under those circumstances?" (John Arlott, The Oval 1948)

One wet February night a couple of years ago we were steaming up the autobahn through Germany on the long haul home to Brussels. Sleek BMWs and Mercedes glided past us on both sides, disappearing into the spray and darkness, on to Bonn, Cologne, Dusseldorf ... it was one of those journeys which seem as if they will never end, as the windscreen wipers swing back and forwards across the darkness and you calculate how many more hours it will still take to get back, if you're lucky.

And then, finally, something snapped. I couldn't listen to the children's *Famous Five* tape any more. To muffled protests from the back, I switched to the radio instead to hear – ah bliss! – Henry Blofeld beaming in loud and strong from Georgetown.

My wife groaned beside me and dug deeper into her coat against both outer gloom and inner despair. Normally I'd have been with her there – I can't stand Henry Blofeld with his false bonhomie and fake, calculating, Bertie Woosterish charm. If I never hear of another bus passing down the Harleyford Road or another pigeon crossing his line of vision it will be too soon. But somehow – oops, there goes Butcher – amid the encircling night, far from home, in driving rain, surrounded by cars going far too fast, there was a little glimmer of sunshine in our car. Blast, that's Hussain gone. Goodness it was hot out there. What a lovely morning. Thank you Henry. Damn, now Thorpe's out.

As I think of it, cricket in Europe is much like that: very English,

The New Ball

a long way away, surrounded by alien indifference. And often very swiftly out.

It is hard to believe, I know, but cricket is actually played in some 30 European countries, apart from England. Cricket in Scotland you'll have heard about, and Holland and Denmark. But Belarus, Estonia, Slovenia? Can you imagine on some hot summer Saturday someone trundling in to bowl from the silver birch tree end in Minsk, or someone else hitting the ball to the Ljubljana boundary? There are some corners of a few foreign fields which are forever, well, these days, as likely to be Karachi, Melbourne, Wellington or Surrey, as Luxembourg or Paris.

Take my club. The Royal Brussels, for all its lofty title, graciously bestowed upon us some years ago by the king of Belgium after we wrote and asked him (his letter of regal approval now hangs behind the pavilion bar), is like thousands of clubs back home. Apart from our matting wicket, all the usual conventions are maintained: tea between innings, 20 overs in the last hour and so on. Our sweaters are embroidered with that tastefully appropriate symbol of Brussels, the Mannekin Pis. And we have a very pretty ground set in the middle of rolling farmland, with a church spire and cottages in the distance, outside the city down towards Waterloo. In fact, you can see the mound that marks the centre of the battlefield in the distance through the trees beyond deep midwicket.

It somehow seems appropriate, given all that guff about the battle in 1815 being won on the playing fields of Eton, that we should play these days so close by. Marshal Blucher's Prussian troops actually marched down the lane to our ground on their way to saving the day for Wellington and making a world safe for Englishmen to play cricket in. Deep in supposed concentration in the field my mind often slips to the scene: Excuse me. Would you mind NOT marching behind the bowler's arm?

THE FIRST CRICKET match played in Belgium is usually thought to have been a knock-up game between Guards officers a week before the battle, in a clearing in the woods nearer Brussels while they waited for Napoleon to turn up. There is some dispute, however: there also appears to have been a game played at Spa, the old health resort in eastern Belgium, as early as 1768. Mind you, in those days that part of the world was part of the Netherlands and owned by the Austrians. In any event, no one plays round there today.

Our team is, as you would expect from the proximity of all the European Union's institutions, highly cosmopolitan. This year's captain happens to be English, but last year's was Pakistani and the year before's Irish. Our bowling is sometimes opened by a quiet Australian and a noisy New Zealander, there's a smattering of South Africans, the ambassadors of Fiji and Gambia have been known to turn out in the past and we also have John Vaughan, the Barbadian who played for Canada in the 1979 World Cup.

But there are very few Belgians. We did have a chap called Erik the Belgian who turned up out of the blue for nets one year and proceeded to bowl like a rocket and straight as an arrow. When asked in awe where he'd learnt to bowl, he modestly replied that he'd never actually turned his arm over before, just picked up the general idea from a Test match on the BBC. But even he isn't about any more. Nor, of course, is Test cricket on the BBC, denying any other likely youngster in our part of Europe a chance of spotting the game being played at international level on television. Soon we won't have it on the radio either. Still, I'm sure it's worth it to Lord's for the money.

One of our few native players is Arnie van Maeterlinck, who gained his enthusiasm for the game while growing up in Oregon of all places, in a city where they actually had the only cricket team for several hundred miles. But as he once said ruefully to me, "cricket isn't really a game which appeals to the Gallic soul." They much prefer baseball, which used to be played on the next field to ours so that French whoops and screams punctured our genteel Saturday afternoon quiet, interspersed with the polite applause and cheery cries of "good shot sir!" from our end of the ground. Very few of the baseball crowd ever paused to watch us on their way to using the toilets in the back of our pavilion.

Periodically, the Belgian press publishes ironical and heavy-humoured articles about this weird game of ours, which lasts for hours and is interrupted for tea. They even try earnestly to explain what goes on: we use *une longue palette de 35 cms*, apparently, to defend *trois petits piquets*. What larks.

Incidentally, during my in-depth research for this article, I learned that the French even have a word for the cricketer's box, presumably brought into use during particularly rough games of petanque. They call it Un Coq. How typical, said the French woman who told me this, that the French word should celebrate masculinity while the English one should seek to enclose it.

Although there's much greater enthusiasm in the Flemish (northern) half of the country, Belgium itself would struggle to raise a team of native-born players, or even the eight required by ECC rules. Holland long since gave up playing us and we haven't put out a side against France for a while. The nearest we get to an international is when the solitary club in Luxembourg comes up to play us, but then, for them, every away game is a foreign tour.

To get to Brussels is a 260-mile round trip and we're the Luxembourg Optimists' nearest opposition, so to play in the Belgian league requires some dedication on their part. The Grand Duchy is now an affiliate member of the International Cricket Council. It slightly inflated its claims to representative status by including two evening teams and the Optimists' women's side to demonstrate the game's popularity there. Nevertheless, cricket receives money from the government as a recognised sport, though no native-born Luxemburger has ever been known to pick up a bat with the possible exception of the country's elderly head of state Grand Duke Jean, who went to school at Ampleforth.

The Belgian league currently has nine teams in its first division and there are a few more sides dotted about. The Hasselt Hedgehogs folded this year, flattened by the ineluctable onrush of a player shortage, but a Pakistani side called Khan, product of yet another split among the local Asian community, is likely to replace them. We already have two Pakistani sides, plus the Antwerp Indians who mainly work in the diamond industry and consequently have enough money to have bought their own ground, a former football stadium in the suburbs.

Thus the Belgian cricket federation is a bona fide body. At our annual meeting last March we gathered as solemnly as any MCC committee to discuss matters of weight and moment, like why the largely Flemish Mechelen Eagles had somehow managed to commandeer the one artificial wicket on offer to Belgium, paid for by the ICC last year (an eye to the main chance and native cunning seemed to have most to do with it as far as everyone else was concerned – none of the other clubs had realised such bounty was on offer). The secretary's report contained a note that exactly one letter had been received all year.

ARE WE UNUSUAL? Perhaps not. I guess most European countries would recognise this parochialism. Behind the rhetoric about how simply splendidly the game is doing on those infrequent occasions when its appearance on the Continent is mentioned, the truth is that it remains a largely expatriate game, thinly spread indeed among the local populations, with little status or profile, not much positive media coverage: an acquired taste for a small, discerning minority rather than a national passion, requiring something close to heroic dedication to follow, with little chance of change. A bit like cricket is becoming in England, really.

Across the border from us in France teams have been sprouting for years – there are currently thought to be 43 clubs and 1,000 players, spread from Antibes on the Riviera to Chauny and St Quentin in the north and St Malo in the west . A thousand, mostly ex-pats, out of a population of 50m, so clearly the game has never really caught on – that Gallic soul thing again. France does, however, have associate status at the ICC, alongside mightier countries such as Scotland, Ireland, Holland and Denmark.

There are more sophisticated explanations for the lack of interest, all about Frenchmen (and other Continentals) not really carrying on with what are regarded as children's games once they grow up – though that takes no account of soccer. The historian GM Trevelyan facetiously reckoned that if the French nobility had played cricket with their servants, as the English squirearchy did, there would have been no revolution. It is indeed true that the 18th-century aristocracy did become dangerously detached from their estates, but that scarcely accounts for why the French don't really play these days.

Yet there are those who argue that the first references to cricket are actually in France. Perhaps it was French shepherds rather than English ones who first tossed knuckle bones at wicket fences. A manuscript from St Omer near Calais in 1478 talks of "criquet" being played in what seems to have been mid-October. Dammit, the French even won the Olympic silver medal in 1900, losing to England at the last Games in which cricket actually featured as a sport (Belgium took the bronze, allegedly). Currently negotiations are on again to get the game recognised, if not necessarily played (not enough countries participate, apparently) by the great panjandrums of the Olympic committee. Somewhat discouragingly, while it featured in the 1998 Commonwealth Games, it has been dropped for the 2002 Games, even if they are taking place in Manchester.

There was, though, a pleasing whiff of the home counties as I tried to catch up with Tom Keeble, the retired doctor who is now secretary of France Cricket, at his home in Conchy-les-Pots near Noyon in the Oise. "He's out umpiring a match. Try tomorrow," his wife told me.

It had been the day of the eclipse. Next day he was back. "We had this Kent side. Came all the way from England, on the ferry in the morning, played cricket all day, back home on the ferry in the evening. They wanted to be able to say 'Total Eclipse Stopped Play' in their scorebook," he chortled. "When I retired in Herefordshire, I umpired my last league match at Monmouth, knowing we were moving to France, and I thought that would be the last cricket ground I'd ever see. How wrong I was – I've done 9,000 kilometres this year, driving to umpire matches. I am the only qualified umpire in France, you see. I feel I have an obligation to be available but it means I spread myself very thin."

To play cricket in many parts of France you do have to be quite dedicated, or hopelessly infatuated, turning out on what are little more than fields, with no changing facilities, at the mercy of municipal park keepers who know even less about groundsmanship than their English counterparts. Vincennes has a particularly vicious reputation. But there are also pretty grounds such as that at the Chateau de Thoiry just outside Paris, tucked away in parkland so extensive it also includes a wildlife park and requires a hike of what seems like miles from the car park to the pitch.

Cricket does have official recognition in France as part of a tri-sport association which also incorporates baseball and softball. And this year it has also been engaged in what is an almost quintessentially Gallic row. The French team was disinvited from the European Colts' tournament in Belfast in July, after coming up with a team for what was essentially an under-19s competition with nine players aged under 15, including one as young as 12, and a girl. The organisers drew the line, all for encouraging youth and all that, but on grounds of safety as much as anything else. Allowing strapping 19-year-olds to bowl competitively at a 12-year-old was not thought a good idea.

"It was a misjudgement, a miscalculation which has now become compounded by their attitude," sniffs Nigel Laughton, the ICC's development officer for Europe at Lord's. "I've seen the 12-year-old. He's perfectly good but not that good – could probably compete at under-14 level. Only a couple of members of the French association can't see it. But we don't want to jeopardise the game in France." There has been a complaint from France and what seems to be mutual incomprehension on both sides.

"The trouble is that once a team has been selected it is illegal to change it in France. The rules about age qualifications for the tournament were not written down," sighs Tom Keeble. "It has soured relations and, even if it is not the biggest crisis in the world, it is a very awkward situation. People are taking positions on both sides which are not very helpful and it is still not resolved."

IN GERMANY, TOO, the game has been played for many years without ever really catching on. The Berlin Cricket Club was founded in the 1850s, the Deutsche Cricket und Fussball Bund was in existence from 1893 and at the start of the First World War there were 14 teams playing in a league around the capital. The Gentlemen of Worcester, including four county players, toured in 1937 and played two "Test" matches but still didn't put Hitler off challenging the might of England. This year it gained associate status of the ICC.

Now there are five regional leagues, from Munich to Hamburg, and 35 teams, though participation is still 80 per cent expatriate: which would mean 100-odd German players from a population of 80m. The departure of British troops has been a blow but, as across most of Europe, there are thriving Asian immigrant teams, some of whom, pleasingly, now play in the grounds of the old Berlin Olympic stadium of 1936, where the Fuhrer is supposed to have snubbed the black American athlete Jesse Owens for showing up his racial superiority theories by winning four golds.

Down in the far south-eastern corner of the country Dr Brian Fell, a lecturer at Passau University and president of the German Cricket Association, is busily labouring to encourage his law students to take up the game, even if it means they have to travel two hours to Munich in one direction or 300 kilometres to Vienna in the other to play a match.

"I took some of my students to England and as we passed The Oval I ordered them to doff their caps," he said. "When they asked why, I told them about cricket and said I'd explain how to play when we got back home. As soon as we got back to Passau they started coming up and asking when they could play. I guess that's how it started.

"It is a game for Anglophiles, though we have our own German terms. LBW translates quite neatly as *forgestandung*, over is *wechsel* – change – and first slip becomes *erstefangman* – first capturer. Funnily enough, bowling comes easier to them than batting. They tend to be too stiff – don't get the idea of moving forward or backwards to the pitch of the ball. They stand still and wait for it to bounce too much before reacting to it."

Let's not get into racial stereotypes here. Across the Alps in Italy there is a far more driven approach which may yet pay dividends with, as in rugby, a national team which is more than the sum of its local parts.

The ambition is for international success and there has been a sort of ruthlessness to compete that is almost wholly the work of one man, Simone Gambino, a Rome estate agent who became besotted with cricket while spending his summers in England with relatives as a child. He is very ambitious for the game in Italy and has put up much of the funding that sustains it in a country where teams stretch from Sicily to the Alps. Italian cricket now has a budget of £100,000 a year, with sponsorship from the likes of Alitalia and the Candy washing machine company. Forty per cent of it is spent just getting the teams to matches.

Expatriates have been sternly excised in the drive to encourage Italians to play, with rules insisting that no two expats can bat, or

Expatriates have been excised to encourage Italians to play: no two expats can bat, or bowl, at the same time

bowl at the same time, and that Italians must come first in the batting order. Italians brought up in Australia are encouraged to come home. Unlike in France or Germany, threequarters of the players hold national passports.

I caught up with Signor Gambino on his mobile phone as the Italian team came off the field at Shenley Park at the end of its match against the MCC during its summer tour of England – a tour which was also going to include games against Wales and a Lancashire XI.

"Yeah, we lost but I am very pleased," he exulted. "We had them 41 for four chasing 218, then Andy Flower of Zimbabwe got 85. They were just too strong. We expect to get thrashed but we are learning and you only learn by losing. The national team is the top priority. My aim is to get into the top playing group in Europe, take on the likes of Holland and Denmark, leave France and Germany behind."

Things are rather different across the Adriatic in Slovenia, though maybe some of the accents are the same. "I caught my interest in the game in seven years in New Zealand," says the Ljubljana club's moving spirit Damir Alidzanovic. "I've been back for three years and the club's been going for two. There's only the one club and about 30 people at the moment."

Nevertheless, they've already found some Australian-born Croatians to come up and play, as well as a team from just over the Austrian border in Klagenfurt. They even enticed the Slovenian president Milan Kucan to come and watch a game which was being broadcast on state television. Slovenia distances itself from the rest of former Yugoslavia – it may be some time before Serbs take up the game.

ALL ACROSS Europe such stirrings are evident. PE teachers at Warsaw's teacher training college have recently been persuaded to try Kwik Cricket. But in a region where the game is never seen on television and scarcely reported in the press, rarely played in schools, with clubs few and far between, it is never going to be a robust flower.

Even in Denmark and Holland, the two countries where the game is strongest, it is still very much a minority, Anglophile occupation. In Denmark there are 3,000 players in a country of 5m people and in Holland maybe 5,000 players and 50 clubs. Both, however, have maximised their resources.

But isn't it very popular? I asked George Moon, captaining the veterans' Still Going Strong side during a break for rain in their annual fixture against us in Brussels. George, who has lived in the Netherlands for 25 years, wrinkled his nose, gazed lightly at the side's Yorkshire-born septuagenarian wicketkeeper – 45 years in Holland – and gave his considered opinion. "Nah, it's very much fathers and sons, the Anglophile middle classes," he said. "If you don't live near a cricket ground or come across it somehow you don't really see it. It's not in the schools, much. Look at us – seven Dutch, an Indonesian, Aftab from Surinam and three English. That would be about usual – the Dutch are probably just in the majority."

Nevertheless, the league structure is strong, particularly around the Hague, Rotterdam and Amsterdam, with teams rich enough to pay young professionals, usually from South Africa and Australia, to coach and play for them. Hylton Ackerman is remembered with great affection, Barry Richards, funnily enough, less so. Four Dutch players (Lefebvre, van Troost, Bakker and Zuiderent) – all but one seam bowlers – have even broken into county cricket.

If the game is thin on the ground, though, its organisation certainly optimises potential – good young players get spotted, coached and taken up into national youth teams, even if some of them are only playing cricket because their dads did before them. The current debate is whether the top league should be expanded to take more clubs, so broadening sponsorship and resources, but at the risk of diluting standards.

There's a new ground with a grass wicket at Amstelveen, where South Africa played Kenya in the World Cup and where Holland will play home internationals in future. It was there that they gave Durham an awful fright this summer, by beating them in the third round of the NatWest Trophy – a landmark day indeed.

On their outings to Holland this summer, the national press's more parochial cricket writers found it awfully funny to think of all the spectators being on the grass – smoking themselves dopey that is, which is all that most cricket writers know about what goes on in the Netherlands. Closer observation might have shown them that the

World Cup match was largely attended by young South Africans, who might well have been trying out the weed.

"There were about 4,000 spectators, most of whom we'd never seen before," says David Hardy, another long-term expatriate. "Anyone who knows anything about Dutch cricket would know they're all terribly Anglophile and formal – it's all collars and ties and Marks and Spencer blazers and standing around drinking tea. Just like at a match in England. Not a lot of dope smoking."

The NatWest tie was much more significant, though only a handful of Dutch spectators turned up to see it. Holland won by five wickets after bowling Durham out for 194. "Durham were crap," said Hardy simply. "They looked as if they'd been on the booze all night. David Boon seemed really shocked. I don't think he could believe it."

If the next round saw Kent bring the Dutch back to earth, they have now beaten representative sides from Australia, South Africa, the West Indies and England, twice, in the past decade. Their quandary now is where to take the game next. Fully professional, so that players can turn out in the week, all summer long, without having to take leave from their jobs? Challenging in county cricket in four-day matches, not just one-day competitions? Is there the money or the interest to do it in Holland? Or is that a bridge too far?

In Denmark, too, there is a similarly strong organisational structure and Anglophile tradition. Here, too, cricket was played even during the Second World War – a small subversive gesture towards the Germans, as in Holland. These days there are about 50 active clubs, playing on matting wickets laid across bases of red clay, producing fast tracks and steepling bounce. No wonder the Danes produce good seamers too.

"Imagine English cricket as it was played 50 years ago – that's us," says Simon Talbot, a former stalwart of Dorset cricket, now Denmark's development officer and coach. "They play very hard but with a good spirit. At the end of the game both teams line up on the boundary to shake hands and the losers buy the beer. These are guys who have played with each other all their lives, they all know each other and they all take the mickey. In England you get a bad attitude; here it is incredibly positive. It is fantastic. I am very happy here."

International sides don't usually penetrate as far as Denmark, which is why the game is not quite as advanced as in Holland – Australia were last to pass through in 1992 – but the Danes may one day have to ask themselves similar questions about the future of the game. The Danes are good at spotting and nurturing talent young, with flourishing under-14 and under-19 sides. For the moment, though, the European future, as Talbot says, is orange.

BACK AT LORD'S Nigel Laughton is sitting on £500,000 to distribute to the game across Europe, for coaching, equipment, facilities, tournaments. He's happy with the way things are going, talking about establishing lift-in and lift-out grass pitches once the technology is perfected over the next few years, grinding his teeth over the loss of television coverage – "we've got no chance until we can get it on the Eurosport channel" – and cheerfully realistic that spreading the game to remote parts is a good in itself, even if Poland and Malta are never going to set Lord's alight.

And yet, and yet. It seems cricket will always remain a minority sport across the Channel. It lacks the roots and the culture. And the coverage. In the first week of September, this year as every year, the Royal Brussels embarked on our annual tour to Kent, playing at Sevenoaks Vine and The Mote at Maidstone, drinking at the Bat and Ball at Leigh near Tonbridge. In Belgium there will never be roots like that – only the roots we take with us there.

A few years back, two elderly women walking their dogs around the boundary where we were playing at Itchenor Park, paused to watch us floundering in the field. They asked who the home side were playing and, when told, nodded sagely and said: "That accounts for it – we thought they couldn't be English ..." ◖

LICENSED TO THRILL SHOAIB AKHTAR GENTLY INFORMS STEPHEN FLEMING HE'S ONE STUMP SHORT OF A WICKET, PAKISTAN v NZ, OLD TRAFFORD

LICENSED TO CHILL STEVE WAUGH PULLS A SIX AGAINST SOUTH AFRICA DURING THE CENTURY THAT KEPT AUSTRALIA IN THE COMPETITION, HEADINGLEY

Colin Shindler
Yorkshire Ruined My Life

Colin Shindler is a TV producer and screenwriter who has revealed much of his Jewish upbringing in Manchester in the Fifties and Sixties in his bestselling autobiography *Manchester United Ruined My Life*, shortlisted for the 1998 William Hill Sports Book of the Year. His first novel, *High on a Cliff*, was published by Headline in August and his second, *Just in Time*, is due out next year. Neither of them, unfortunately, mention Brian Statham.

Wickedest wicket Jack Bond's flying catch. Asif Iqbal c Bond b Simmons 89. Lancashire beat Kent by 24 runs to take the Gillette Cup at Lord's, September 1971.

Soundest bite "We're not going to let the New Zealand bowlers dominate us; we're going to take the attack to them and try and survive the first hour." (Nasser Hussain, July 1999)

It is a belief in Yorkshire that 1999 is the 150th anniversary of the first Roses match, two of which, they claim, were played in 1849. Both, remarkably, were won by Yorkshire under the captaincy of the Mayor of Sheffield (history does not record if he wore his chain of office on the field of play). I say "remarkably" because Lancashire as a county cricket club was not formed until 1864. This kind of knavery is entirely typical of Yorkshire folk.

The 1999 Roses match thankfully respected one of the great traditions of this, the most traditional of all county championship matches: rain prevented any play before lunch on the first day. That was the end of the ritual. Play commenced shortly before 3pm. Just after tea, Yorkshire were, to widespread astonishment, all out for just 67 in an innings in which there were four hat-trick balls.

Andrew Flintoff then hit a brutal but spectacular 160 out of 314 (well, the lad's only 21, he doesn't understand what the Roses match is all about) and Yorkshire subsided tamely by 10 wickets soon after lunch on the third day. It was their third defeat by Lancashire in 10 days, adequate compensation for their victory at Old Trafford in a keenly-fought NatWest quarter-final at the end of July. Lancashire glided above Yorkshire into fourth place in the championship. I trust I have made my allegiance perfectly clear.

The victory should have filled me with deep satisfaction but throughout the match I was conscious of a cloying melancholy which was unrelated to the despair being felt at the same time by the woman steward in Stand C. As I stood to applaud Richard Green's dismissal of Craig White which reduced the Auld Enemy to a humiliating 27 for six, she looked sourly at me. "We're going to win this one in two days," I exulted. "We don't get paid if it finishes early," she complained. "And put that bloody phone away, you'll get me the sack," she added, as I started to dial my son with the glad tidings.

Whence came this melancholy? The real reason is an unashamedly romantic one. There was, for a county game, a fair-sized crowd of maybe a couple of thousand but in a ground designed to hold 10 times that number the empty spaces echoed with the sounds of yesteryear. I felt as if I were the embodiment of the spirit of Neville Cardus who had sat through all three days of the 1926 match before a crowd that totalled 78,617. On August Bank Holiday Monday, in front of the all-time record of 46,000, Lancashire passed 500 for the first time against Yorkshire. Needless to say the match was drawn and the battle was fought solely over the destination of first-innings points. We won.

THE WHITSUNTIDE Lancashire v Yorkshire match of 1955 was the first county game I ever saw. I have only two memories (I was five years old) of this significant event. The first was being told that the old man trotting to his place in the slips was none other than Len Hutton, the England captain who had recently returned from his triumphant tour of Australia where the Ashes had been gloriously retained, thanks to Brian Statham and a few other names I couldn't absorb.

Sadly, I have no memory of Cyril Washbrook's fighting innings of 70 which steadied the Lancashire first innings but I can see now the splayed stumps as the great Hutton, Yorkshire's champion for the past 20 years, was clean bowled for two. The successful bowler was KB Standring, a local grammar school boy who played for Clitheroe in the Ribblesdale League. He played only five more matches for the county before fading from view but that heroic delivery has cemented his place in my heart.

The Roses matches, I was grimly informed, were more important than any other fixture played over the course of an English summer. To lose to Yorkshire was a disgrace much harder to bear than defeat in a Test series. Long before Geoffrey Boycott articulated the feeling, as we watched Fred Trueman running in to bowl at our batsmen, my older brother Geoffrey would warn me constantly that a score of 101 for two was illusory. We had better get used to the idea of its being 101 for four because such a prognostication tended to be based on grim reality.

Even if Statham and Higgs had made inroads into a strong Yorkshire batting order and we had reduced them to 130 for six or thereabouts, somebody would stick around in the lower order. Jimmy Binks and Vic Wilson or Ray Illingworth and Bob Appleyard would get them up to 250 and then there was always the fear that Trueman would rip apart the top half of our batting. If Lancashire beat Yorkshire I didn't mind quite so much if England struggled. In a strange, undefined way, Test matches belonged to Brian Johnston and Peter West. We didn't see much of those Southerners when "real" cricket was being played. That might sound astonishingly parochial today but the fact remains that my relationship with Peter May and Trueman was dictated by the love of my county which was in full bloom from the moment that Standring bowled Hutton.

I recognised that May was arguably the best batsman in the world in the second half of the Fifties and that Trueman was the fastest though not the best bowler in England (vide. JB Statham) and I was glad that they were English during the Test series. However, the truth is that even when Trueman was steaming in against the Australians he was always the "enemy", the Yorkshire opening bowler whose venom was traditionally reserved for "Noddy" Pullar, Ken Grieves and Alan Wharton.

Just as I take a perverse delight in watching Manchester United players being sent off while playing for England (or, better still, spending the night in the cells charged with various offences of public affray) so I preferred to see Statham, or indeed any other bowler, take wickets before Trueman. It appeared to my brother and me, that it was invariably Trueman who was bowling as numbers nine, 10 and 11 came to the wicket. Statham, on the other hand, was held back until a batsman had reached 98 at which point he was handed the ball to ensure that BBC News that night could show the nation that it was off Statham's bowling that the batsman in form reached his century. You will no doubt have concluded by now that I am a prejudiced Lancastrian first and last. Guilty as charged, m'lud.

It was slightly different with May. When I looked at his plastered side parting I saw only the man who scored centuries against Lancashire with such monotonous regularity that we always felt it would have been simpler if he had been officially awarded 112 before the start of play on the first day, after which a relatively competitive championship match could take place between 21 mortals. It was May's sublime batting as much as the havoc created by Tony Lock and Jim Laker that was responsible for Yorkshire suffering a biblical seven years of torment in the Fifties as Surrey retained their exclusive hold on the title. I didn't mind that Surrey won the championship as long as Yorkshire didn't. When Ronnie Burnett's side finally regained the coveted crown in 1959 after 13 barren years I found Lancashire's failings became considerably more painful.

THIS WAS WHY the August Bank Holiday match at Old Trafford in 1960, unarguably one of the greatest of all Roses matches, left such a profound impression on me. Lancashire hosted Yorkshire having already defeated them earlier that season on an atypically dusty wicket at Headingley by 10 wickets, the champions submitting tamely to the broad bat of Pullar and the wrist-spin of Tommy Greenhough and Bob Barber. Yorkshire arrived at Old Trafford second in the table behind a resurgent and confident Lancashire. We didn't necessarily need the artificial competition of points to stiffen the sinews but there is no doubt that the respective placings of the two counties added yet more fuel to the traditional fire.

My uncle Laurence, who had been taking me to watch Lancashire since the day of the Standring incident, had recently moved to London and this was the first Roses match I was permitted to attend without adult supervision. The three days attracted 74,000 spectators, the largest such attendance since the 1926 record – a fitting tribute to the joint beneficiaries, the long-serving spinners Malcolm Hilton and Roy Tattersall whom the parsimonious Lancashire committee (presumably with the tacit approval of the all-powerful Washbrook) had slighted by refusing them richly-deserved individual benefits.

There were no celebrity pro-am golf tournaments and gala dinners to help the beneficiaries in those days and the professionals were almost totally reliant on the gate receipts from the big match for their future livelihood. Lancashire had famously destroyed that of Bertie Buse in 1953 by defeating Somerset by an innings on the first day (Tattersall 13 for 79), bowling them out a second time an hour before the scheduled close. The Somerset committee feeling somewhat guilty offered Buse another match but the old pro, who had already paid out certain fixed costs, declined with thanks, saying he couldn't afford it.

The 1960 Roses match at Old Trafford was the most exciting county match I have ever seen. Statistically you can argue that it was no more exciting than any other game in which victory is achieved off the last ball. One-day cricket has produced numerous examples; Lancashire and Yorkshire contrived one such mighty climax in a B&H Cup semi-final in 1996 when Peter Martin scooped the last ball from Craig White past point for two, having been unable to lay bat on either of the fourth or fifth balls of the final over. To me, however, such finishes, though unquestionably exciting, are somehow less worthy than those which culminate at the end of a three-, four- or five-day, two-innings affair because the artificial format of the one-day game facilitates, indeed, positively encourages such a conclusion.

The late Fifties and early Sixties were punctuated by constant calls for "Brighter Cricket" though quite what that meant nobody ever really defined. After the high point of attendances in the late Forties county cricket embarked on its steep decline which has resulted in players performing in front of achingly empty terraces whilst the enthusiasts to whom county cricket still means something, follow the play on Teletext or the internet. The Roses match, however, still managed to attract large crowds well after the decline had set in. In 1954 there were 29,000 at Headingley on the Monday and as late as 1966 24,000 were estimated to be at Leeds on the first two days to watch Brian Close's Yorkshire in their pomp.

That 1960 Roses match asssumes a significance in my mind greater perhaps than its true importance to the destination of the championship, because it was one of very few matches I have ever attended in which I felt linked to the tradition of county cricket when the championship mattered because it was the only trophy to be played for. It can be argued that Roses matches, perhaps up to the late Sixties when Lancashire developed into a very good one-day side under Jack Bond, were the last to preserve that tradition. Thereafter the crowds came out to watch county matches only in their abbreviated guise. Indeed, the Lancashire v Yorkshire John Player League match at the end of August 1970, which Lancashire won to retain the trophy in the second year of its existence, remains the only Lancashire game I have ever travelled to and been locked out of because the turnstiles had closed with the ground full. The supremacy of the one-day game has remained unchallenged since that time. These days, the nearest we will ever get to the Roses matches of my youth would be if the protagonists met in a Lord's final.

WHEN YORKSHIRE came to Old Trafford over the 1960 August Bank Holiday weekend Lancashire had won two out of the sides' last three meetings – heady success indeed in Roses matches, whose tradition had contained far more draws and Yorkshire wins than was good for the health of my family. Vic Wilson's men arrived grimly determined to extract revenge for the defeat at Headingley in May.

They didn't make much of a fist of it on the Saturday. Bob Barber and Wharton carried Lancashire past the Yorkshire first-innings score with only one wicket down but Trueman and Mel Ryan restricted the eventual lead to 72. When Statham and Higgs removed half the Yorkshire side for 36 it seemed likely we would be celebrating a rare innings victory. Led by Phil Sharpe, the best slip catcher I ever saw, Yorkshire recovered to 149 but that still left Lancashire to score a mere 78 in over two hours after lunch on the Tuesday afternoon. Time to unravel the bunting? In your dreams.

Lancashire wickets seemed to fall more regularly than runs were scored and after an hour and a half they were marooned on 43 for six. As so often in the past, the Australian Grieves marshalled the rearguard action and the score crept agonisingly up towards the target. At 60 Grieves miscued Trueman straight to Wilson at deep mid-off. Wilson was one of the safest catchers in England. We groaned as the ball dropped safely into those massive hands of his – and out again to a triumphant roar. Trueman's grand tragic gesture of despair only increased our happiness.

However, with only two overs left we still needed 18 – laughable in the context of today's one-day cricket but a veritable mountain on that hot August day. Geoff Clayton, known as "Chimp" because of his monkey-like crouch behind the wicket, fluked two edgy fours off Ryan but the cries of ecstasy were stilled as Grieves nicked one to Binks and was caught. At the start of the final over, to be bowled (with dramatic aptness) by Trueman, there were three wickets left and six runs needed.

Clayton was left with the dilemma of protecting the tail or taking every run on offer. Off the first ball he pushed a single and opted to take it. A wise decision we thought. Greenhough could handle a bat and it was one less to get. Off the second Trueman uprooted Greenhough's leg stump. What an idiot Clayton was to have taken that single, screamed 12,000 Lancastrians. Jack Dyson, the off-spinner and Manchester City forward whose job I coveted, came in to join Clayton and scrambled two improbable leg-byes off his first ball. Three to win, three balls to go, two wickets left.

Dyson just dug Trueman's fourth ball out of the blockhole, looked up expecting to see Clayton's beam of approval only to find his partner galloping towards him screaming the same words as everybody else in the crowd. Dyson just made his ground in a flurry of bodies, bat and broken stumps. Clayton drove a single off the penultimate ball which meant that we couldn't lose. That wasn't much comfort since for all but the last two hours Lancashire had been winning the match since the first ball. A draw now would be desperately disappointing.

The fielders closed in. Trueman stamped back to his mark. Dyson looked round the field. It was hard to see where that run was going to come from. There seemed to be no gaps anywhere. Contracts with God were being rapidly made all round the ground as Trueman steamed in. Gathering pace he launched himself at the popping crease, the ball aimed unerringly for another middle-stump yorker. At the last moment it started swinging to leg, Dyson got a thick inside edge and the ball shot away past backward short leg and

The Wars of
were **fought,**
blue plaque on
St. Albans
distinguished
double yellow
zealous traffic
anxious to mai

the Roses

according to a

the site of

Library,

today by

lines and

wardens

tain hostilities

over the boundary at deep fine leg. The crowd erupted and spilled onto the pitch. The stentorian voice of the Lancashire secretary issued his traditional but now futile demand over the loudspeaker, "Would the little boys please keep off the pitch", but he was doomed to disappointment. I was 11 years old and I had found my drug of choice.

MEMORIES of great Roses clashes thereafter are patchy. Lancashire rapidly descended into the lower depths of the table as a series of defeats and well-publicised rows tore the club apart. In August 1964, Peter Marner, Clayton, Grieves and Dyson were uncerominiously sacked by a committee who had already driven Wharton to seek sanctuary at Leicestershire and Barber at Warwickshire. Statham and Higgs continued to be one of the best new-ball partnerships in first-class cricket but you couldn't expect to lose players like that and still be competitive with Yorkshire. Admittedly, the Tykes had lost Willie Watson and Dickie Bird to Leicestershire and Johnny Wardle to the fury of their own committee but Brian Bolus, who opened for England, had to move to Nottinghamshire to assure himself of regular first-team action so strong were Yorkshire throughout the Sixties.

Before Clive Lloyd and Farokh Engineer arrived to form the backbone of Bond's successful one-day side Lancashire were no match for the Yorkshire of Trueman, Close, Illingworth and Nicholson in their pomp and I was reduced to finding solace in learning about the history of the Roses matches and quite why they mattered so much.

For Shakespeare the seeds of the conflict were sewn in the Temple garden early in the 15th century. In Act II scene IV of Henry IV Part One, the Duke of Somerset plucks a red rose from a nearby bush to signify his support of the Lancastrian King. Richard Plantaganet, with typical Yorkshire not to say Boycottian contrariness, decides that because he is descended from an older son of Edward III and anyway, Henry IV had illegally usurped the throne from the murdered Richard II, his claim to the throne of England is the superior one. He promises no flashy stuff as a future king, just a lot of hard graft and sound defensive policies.

In somewhat heightened verse Richard of York bemoans the vagaries of the selectors, who must, since this was the age of the Divine Right of Kings, have included God. At least, from a Lancastrian perspective, this lays to rest their traditional boast that God is a Yorkshireman. To indicate his own feelings about the Royal Selector and his support of Yorkshire, the Earl of Warwick, presumably an ancestor of MJK Smith, plucks a white rose as he aligns himself with Richard Hutton-Plantaganet, Duke of York.

The Wars of the Roses are therewith born, though a more entertaining version is championed by Mel Brooks's 2,000 Year-Old Man who attributes the origins of the conflict to a deficiency of deodorants. Roses therefore become the only means available for human beings to smell acceptably and are consequently fought over bitterly by all parties ("Hey, don't you smell my roses, Mister!").

It's certainly true that the Wars of the Roses were fought all over England, including, according to a blue plaque on the site which was extant when I was living in the town, the St. Albans Public Library, a battlefield distinguished today by double yellow lines and zealous traffic wardens anxious to maintain a history of hostilities.

The narrative of Shakespeare's history plays was mostly taken from Holinshed's Chronicles. If only he had read Cardus. What a list of dramatis personae we might then have had. The lordly Archie MacLaren and Lord Hawke, the lyrical artist Reggie Spooner, the dashing romantic JT Tyldesley, the Honourable FS Jackson and the imperturbable Herbert Sutcliffe would obviously have spoken in glorious iambic pentameters. The workaday professionals on the other hand, Harry Makepeace and Ernest Tyldesley of Lancashire and Wilfred Rhodes and Emmott Robinson of Yorkshire, would have played the comedy parts and spoken in plain prose. How the groundlings would have roared at the bon mots of those doughty old pros – "What we want in Yarksheer and Lankysheer matches is fair do's – no umpires and fair cheatin' all round."

That, allegedly, was the voice of Roy Kilner, the Yorkshire all-rounder who sadly died of a disease contracted on a tour of India in 1928. We believe that is the way he spoke because Cardus tells us that is how he spoke. Cardus also tells us of a conversation between Rhodes and Robinson inspecting a rain-affected wicket in

Bradford. "Tek spin around four," opines the old maestro Rhodes. "Nay, Wilfred," replies Robinson, shocked at his partner's vagueness, "quarter past!"

That one is my favourite but the stories are many and legion. Emmott Robinson was never remotely considered good enough to play for England but according to Cardus he epitomised the spirit of his county. God created him in the manner more traditionally reserved for Adam by scooping up the nearest acre of Yorkshire soil at hand and breathing into it saying, "Now, lad, tha's called Emmott Robinson and tha' can go on with t' new ball at t' pavilion end." Robinson would carry the new ball in his hands between overs, handing it over to the other opening bowler with care as if delivering a priceless but fragile artefact, lest some ignorant novice spoil it by throwing it along the ground.

Robinson and Rhodes ran the Yorkshire team in the Twenties as a joint dictatorship. The captain, a pleasant individual called Major Lupton, was allowed to toss the coin at the start of play; otherwise his function was purely ceremonial. On the final day of one match, Yorkshire were progressing comfortably enough towards a declaration when a wicket fell. Major Lupton disappeared into the amateurs' dressing room to pad up. When he emerged he was greeted by Robinson with the short statement, " I shouldn't bother if I were thee, Major. Wilfred's declaring end of t' next over."

Robinson and Rhodes had one of their finest hours at the end of the August Bank Holiday Roses match in August 1922. In a low-scoring game Yorkshire had taken first-innings points by a matter of four runs. Lancashire struggled to 135 in their second innings leaving Yorkshire to score 132 to win. Apart from Robinson and Rhodes only Percy Holmes had managed to get into double figures. At the start of the final over to be delivered by Cec Parkin, Yorkshire needed five to win but had only one wicket left. How different this over was to be from the similar situation facing Lancashire in 1960.

Parkin's first four balls were played back to the bowler by Rhodes who had no interest in taking runs that would leave "Abe" Waddington, the no.11, to face Lancashire's best bowler. The packed crowd roared Parkin on for one last mighty effort. They roared too loud. The fifth ball was a no-ball. Rhodes could now win with one lusty immortal blow to the boundary. Did he try? Did he blazes. The fifth legitimate delivery was played immaculately back to the bowler. The sixth produced one run to third man. The match was drawn. The possibility of victory in a Roses match was as naught compared with the calamity of defeat. Rhodes knew his duty.

THE TWO DECADES between the wars epitomised the kind of attritional cricket we Northerners conjure up when we refer to the Roses matches. This was partly due to the quality of the two teams. In the 18 seasons from 1922 to 1939 Yorkshire won the championship 11 times, Lancashire five. Only Nottinghamshire in 1929 and Derbyshire in 1936 halted this irresistible tide of Northern domination. Each Roses match was played not just for local pride but also for vital points which led to the belief that first-innings points in a drawn game were almost as good as a victory.

Those people who saw in such drawn games nothing but dull cricket (they invariably originated south of a line drawn across the country and passing through Sheffield) missed the point of Roses matches. Rumours abounded that no batsman should ever cut before lunch or drive before tea on the first day and that it would be better all round if boundaries were eschewed altogether.

It wasn't that the batsmen couldn't score quickly. Any batting order which included Paynter, Washbrook, Tyldesley (E) and Hopwood on the one side and Holmes, Sutcliffe, Leyland and Kilner on the other was perfectly capable of scoring quickly. In Roses matches the point was not getting out rather than scoring runs, frustrating the opposition rather than offering them the slightest glimmer of an opening. In statistical terms, between 1919 and 1939, Yorkshire scored their runs in the Roses matches at the deadly slow rate of 2.45 runs per over; Lancashire managed 2.07.

Cardus describes one such passage of play so definitively that it is worth quoting in full.

Imagine the scene: Bramall Lane. Factory chimneys everywhere; a pall of smoke between earth and sun. A crowd mainly silent; hard hats or caps and scarves on all sides. Harry Makepeace is facing Rhodes; old soldier against old soldier. Makepeace has only one purpose in life at the moment, and that is not to get out. And Rhodes pitches a ball wide of the off-stump – pitches it there so that Makepeace cannot score safely off it. Makepeace, mind you, is not going to put his bat anywhere near a ball if he can help it ... Appeals for leg-before-wicket [are] the only signs of waking life for hours.

It is a more romantic description of the sort of cricket which induced from one Lancastrian, frustrated by an interminable stonewalling display from Sutcliffe, the plaintive cry, "'Erbert, coom on; what dost tha think thi are, a bloody war memorial?"

Between the wars Cardus reported for the *Manchester Guardian* on all 42 Roses matches. His writing was so distinctive that it shaped the entire mythology of these games. The characters he lionised – Rhodes and Robinson, Makepeace and George Duckworth, the Lancashire and England wicketkeeper whose stentorian appeals were the curse of umpires everywhere – remarked later that though they didn't exactly recognise the dialogue he put in their mouths they approved of their sentiments.

It is Cardus whom we must thank for his portraits of Yorkshire and Lancashire characters of the Golden Age. For Cardus there was never an opening trio to compare with MacLaren, Spooner and Johnny Tyldesley, the heroes of his own boyhood. Who now remembers Walter Brearley, Lancashire's greatest fast bowler in the seasons before 1914? Only Cardus records how Brearley trapped George Hirst plumb in front only to have his appeal turned down flat. Hirst then hits Brearley for six off each of the next two balls at which Brearley, bowling even faster, knocks Hirst's middle stump out of the ground, breaking it in two. Brearley races off the ground, seizes six new stumps and brings them back onto the field before the next batsman can take guard. "Here," he says to the umpire, "Tek these. Tha'll need all bloody lot before ah've done." Brearley, according to Cardus, finished the anecdote with a satisfied, "And he needed four of 'em, ah can tell thee."

The Roses matches were heightened as drama because we, the spectators, felt that, like Brearley, the players similarly cared more about beating Yorkshire than any other county. Washbrook was competitive with Hutton, Trueman with Statham, Maurice Leyland with Ernest Tyldesley. Rhodes desperately wanted Makepeace's wicket, Ted Macdonald felt the same about Sutcliffe and everyone wanted to get Hutton out.

Yorkshire were like your next-door neighbour, familiar and constantly irritating. Travelling across the Pennines for the Whitsuntide match at Sheffield we found ourselves in a weird land where everything was the same but everything was different. It was like going next door in a semi-detached house where every room was a confusing mirror image of your own. There were the mills and the factories and the ugly little cricket ground perched precariously under the railway line from which steam belched every over. You recognised Yorkshire people because they came from the same world but they spoke with a different accent, again at the same time both familiar and odd. The rest of England was a different country altogether. It was pretty in a way we didn't recognise. Our countryside was stark in its grandeur. The south of England was where you went on your summer holiday.

WHAT KILLED THE ROSES MATCHES was the M62. Before the motorway was built there was always the fear that you could get cut off crossing the Pennines. Once you left Lancashire you were confronted with a limited number of roads to cross into Yorkshire, usually over the Snake Pass or the Woodhead Pass. At the foot of the moors as the gradient inclined steeply stood a notice indicating whether the road was open or not. You ignored a "Closed" sign at your peril.

Admittedly, it was rare to be stranded on the moors during the cricket season but legends had been created on those lonely hills and the "safety" of Leeds, Sheffield or Bradford town centre could seem a long way off on a dark winter's day in the Fifties. Once the motorway was built it changed the concept of travelling across the Pennines. It was a matter of less than an hour from Headingley to Old Trafford. Yorkshire folk could be seen on the streets of Manchester as a matter of course rather than as a crowd on its way to Old Trafford or the relatively benign Irish Sea off the west coast of Lancashire.

Watching a superficially strong Lancashire team with half a dozen international players in the side take the field against Yorkshire in

The New Ball

August 1999 my mind retreats 40 years and aches again to see the heroes of my youth, too. There is no way in which Pullar, Wharton and Marner can match up to Cardus's legendary trio but I would love to see Statham just once more as in days of yore, white shirt billowing as he begins his smooth acceleration from the Stretford end, the high windmill action of the delivery stride and the vicious breakback as the ball pitches just outside the off stump, beats the tentative forward prod and sends the middle stump cartwheeling. I would, however, settle for Hilton and Tattersall on a helpful pitch bowling to Yorkshire tottering on 65 for five, with the famous predatory close fielders, Grieves, Jack Ikin and Geoff Edrich, clustered round the bat.

Cricket as a game lends itself better than most to the rosy hues of nostalgia, cloaked as they invariably are in the dark shadows cast by the blazing sun of high summer. I have no doubt that my son David will tell his children of the flashing blade of Neil Fairbrother, of the Oriental mysteries of the magical spinner Muttiah Muralitharan and of the broadsword of that youthful giant Flintoff. His memories, though, will be of one-day finals at Lord's against many teams but none of them Yorkshire. Or, even worse, of triumphs seen through the all-pervasive eye of the television camera. Time will only enhance the memory of the wit of Ian Austin and the beamer Wasim Akram launched at Chris Adams.

In 1921 Cardus wrote a report of the Whitsuntide match at Old Trafford which bitterly criticised Lancashire's slow scoring on a perfect pitch. After three and a half hours, he complained, Lancashire had crawled to 140 for one. What would MacLaren or JT Tyldesley have given us of flashing boundaries in like circumstances, he bemoaned. The first six in the Lancashire batting order read Makepeace, Hallows, Ernest Tyldesley, Sharp, Spooner and James Tyldesley. Even Watkinson, Chilton and Lloyd might struggle to get into that lineup.

It wasn't as if the Yorkshire bowling was anything to fear that distant May day as the sun dappled Old Trafford, presenting what Cardus termed "an artist's arrangement in red, white and green and the proud pavilion looked down on us with the air of a living but venerable presence, mellow with age and majestic because it remembered a mighty past". One bowler was barely turning the ball, another turning it so slowly "as not to trouble a first-class cricketer". The two opening bowlers were "penny plain". The first-change bowler was "hardly above good club level". In order of appearance this rubbish was delivered by Wilfred Rhodes, Roy Kilner, Emmott Robinson, Abe Waddington and George Macaulay.

Of course, Washbrook thought Hilton couldn't bowl and Tattersall couldn't spin the ball. As Yorkshire attempted to fight back on the second evening of the 1999 match it was apparent that David Byas thought it was good to see this historic tradition of complete and utter tosh being continued by Glen Chapple and Peter Martin. The trouble with Roses matches is they're never as good as they used to be. ◗

PREMATURE EJACULATOR ALLAN DONALD (LEFT) CELEBRATES A TAD EARLY AS HERSCHELLE GIBBS SPARES STEVE WAUGH, HEADINGLEY

COME AGAIN DONALD (RIGHT) AFTER HIS RUN OUT AGAINST AUSTRALIA HAD RUNG THE CURTAIN DOWN ON ONE-DAY CRICKET'S MOST MESMERIC HOUR, EDGBASTON

Andrew Shields

No Beck's Please, We're British

Andrew Shields is chairman
and fixture secretary of a
medium-sized, multi-racial
cricket club in Essex, and a
qualified coach. In his spare time
he is sports editor of *Time Out*
and the author of three books,
including the football bestseller
The Lad Done Bad.

Wickedest wicket Warne to
Gatting, 1993. The look of utter
bemusement on Gatt's face
creases me up every time I see a
photo of "The Ball from Hell".

Soundest bite "If you're going
to lose, you might as well lose
good and proper and try to sneak
a win." (Ted Dexter, in a rare
moment of verbal inspiration)

The first beamer could have been an accident, of course. Even the best bowlers let one slip now and then, don't they? All it needed was a shout of "sorry, mate" to the other end, or an apologetic wave of the hand, and the throat-high ball would have been forgotten as a fluke. But when a second came straight after, and Terry's follow-through took him to within punching distance of the batsman, it quickly dawned that the deliveries were deliberate.

"Tel! Leave it out!" called the captain, running in from mid-off. The bowler slowly turned and strutted back to his mark. The next ball was quick by anyone's standards – just short of a length, it jagged wickedly into the batsman's ribs. "Fucking hit that!" came the sneering cry down the pitch.

Good bowler but an awkward cuss, old Terence. In fact, if only his attitude would improve he'd be in the 1st XI every week. The captain should have hauled him out of the attack there and then, posted him at fine leg to calm down. But he didn't, and the next over was when it kicked off. This was not "attitude"; this was something altogether nastier.

Had the batsman not been dropping to his knees when Terry was barely into his delivery stride, the third beamer would certainly have achieved the desired effect. Loud Urdu remonstrations poured from the pavilion while the non-striker charged up the pitch to intervene, swinging his bat above his head like a demented hammer-thrower.

"What was that? Eh? Eh?" screamed Tel, his face contorted with rage. "Want some more, you Paki bastards?"

The skipper would have sent him from the field had Terry not swaggered off himself, and gone home without uttering another word. It was the last match he ever played for the club.

Six months later, Terry joined the police force. True story.

I CAN VOUCH for the truth of that vile tale, because I was playing in the game myself. It was June 1991, a fixture in one of the smaller Essex county leagues against an all-Asian side. In more than 25 years of club cricket, it is the only time I have witnessed racial abuse on the pitch and I will never forget the steady build-up and sudden explosion of animosity. Terry's personality made him difficult to talk to and, with hindsight, he should never have been selected for that particular match. Most people were aware that he wasn't terribly keen on those of a different skin colour, though no-one knew the depth of his hatred. When our opponents chose to make obeisance to Mecca as part of their pre-match routine, most of our team looked on with curiosity. Afterwards, we realised it was a gesture almost guaranteed to inflame someone with the poison of prejudice in their blood.

But then the game was being played in Essex. And doesn't this sort of thing happen there all the time? Popular misconception would have it so. This is a county whose image is little more than a collection of cliches: *Birds of a Feather*, Chigwell, the Basildon "badlands", "Billericay Dickie", large ethnic communities rubbing up against the lumpen white working classes. Yet Essex is a county which ill-deserves its reputation.

Its men are routinely mocked as gorblimey caricatures from an old Ian Dury song, while the supposed shallowness of its women's intellect is celebrated in jokes aplenty. Don't bother to look at the school league tables, then, or search for Essex's surprisingly rural charm. Michael Henderson, writing in the *Daily Telegraph*, described Southend as "not the sort of place you visit willingly" and Essex as "surely the least interesting county in England". Undoubtedly, if you confine your visits to press boxes at minor cricketing outgrounds.

It was the reaction to Matthew Engel's editorial in the 1999 *Wisden* which prompted the most malign misrepresentations. Discussing English cricket's failure to embrace the offspring of parents who came to Britain in the wave of postwar migration from the subcontinent and Caribbean, Engel touched on the findings of a report, "Anyone for Cricket?", which examined the culture of the game in Essex and east London. "In an informal, unspoken, very English way, cricketing apartheid has become accepted practice," he wrote. "There is clear-cut evidence of segregation operating, informally, in Yorkshire and Essex. The effect is that black and Asian players have become second-class in all kinds of little ways."

Most follow-up reports mentioned that the situation in Yorkshire was already well known. As for Essex – well, what would you expect?

"ANYONE FOR CRICKET?" was launched at Lord's in May 1998, on the day that the South African tourists arrived for their first net practice. Toting kitbags and hiding behind hats and shades, they looked every inch the modern-day cricket squad, heads down and focused on the task ahead. But as they turned towards the Nursery Ground, around 100 children seated on the steps of the indoor school, multi-racial boys and girls from east London, burst into spontaneous applause. The players, to their credit, acknowledged the cheers; the youngsters, for their part, had unwittingly shown that nationality and skin colour count for nothing. These guys were heroes for one reason only: because they're great cricket players.

It was a heartwarming moment during a heavy morning, spent hearing of discrimination and a widespread failure to understand how black and Asian cricketers want to play the game. The report was commissioned by the London Community Cricket Association and, crucially, the Essex Cricket Association (ECA) – a sharp retort to those who would portray the county in sombre light. The research was carried out in response to figures showing that many clubs with predominantly black and Asian players operate outside the game's established structures: in the Ilford & District region, with the largest non-white population in the county, just 37 out of 90 known clubs are affiliated to the ECA.

In seeking explanation from players, officials and umpires, the researchers found two distinct cricketing "cultures" operating in the area. Black and Asian cricket is played in urban surroundings on poor council-maintained pitches, in a fiercely competitive atmosphere with the result carrying great importance. In contrast, white cricket is played in more rural settings on private grounds, with the traditional rituals of tea and beer strongly to the fore.

Gross generalisations? Of course. But the report does show how unequal these two "cultures" are. Co-author Ian McDonald goes further. He argues that "the white clubs have the power to effect the exclusion of black and Asian teams from the official leagues" – despite an overwhelming desire by those teams to gain recognition. The result is cricket in the region becoming "segregated along the lines of ethnicity", with a "culture of exclusion perpetuated by the established clubs and leagues".

Predictably enough, Matthew Engel's brief analysis in *Wisden* was quickly misinterpreted by sections of the media sniffing a chance to have a pop at Essex: now it was to be labelled the racist county. Instead of being asked to commend the ECA for taking this bold and controversial initiative, various club officials found themselves fending off a succession of bouncers from the media. But in the London morning freesheet *Metro*, the captain of Chingford Cricket Club offered stout defence: actually, half of our 1st XI are black and Asian, he retorted.

Even the briefest scan through the sports pages of the *Ilford Recorder* would confirm this: the teams fielded by what "Anyone for Cricket?" terms the "white establishment" – the 100-year-old clubs with good facilities playing in the top leagues – are, in fact, largely multi-racial. Ability is a far greater concern than skin colour to coaches perpetually searching for the best local talent.

These clubs would point to the multi-racial composition of their teams as evidence that cricket in Essex is not racist. And up to a point they would be justified in doing so. However, black and Asian cricketers want to be accepted not only as skilled individuals, but as whole teams representing a particular way of playing the game. And that is where the clubs' argument weakens. One Asian respondent in "Anyone for Cricket?" articulated the point perfectly:

"Established clubs say, 'Your best players can come and play for us, but no, you can't play in our league'."

"The reason our clubs can't get into their sort of structure is because of the rules," said another Asian player. "You don't have a sightscreen. There isn't a bar. Silly rules to stop you." An Afro-Caribbean official claimed that even when black and Asian clubs do meet the requirements, further obstacles are presented: "Other clubs don't have the facilities we have. Yet they are in the league."

According to many of those questioned, the only solution is to forget about sightscreens and bars, and simply create a huge pyramid system throughout the county. It's a great idea in theory – every team, no matter its resources, has a chance to find its own level. But to insist that existing league structures be demolished in order to accommodate black and Asian clubs running just one team is probably beyond the Essex Cricket Board – and any other Cricket Board, for that matter.

There is, however, one striking example of what would appear to be discrimination. When, in 1997, the top-grade Essex County League vetoed the creation of a third division, this was generally accepted as weaker clubs in division two refusing to vote for their own relegation, rather than a ploy to keep out two clubs which were among the proposed members – one Asian, the other mainly Afro-Caribbean. But when the second-tier Morrant League expanded a year later, and took in all the original applicants to the Essex County League except the Asian and Afro-Caribbean clubs, then one is at least entitled to speculate on the motives for doing so.

OCTOBER 1998, NEWHAM TOWN HALL in the heart of east London. The annual presentation evening for the Gujarati Muslim League. Above the stage, a large banner lists the league's eight sponsors; the competition handbook is full of lucrative advertising, along with detailed fixture and umpire lists and contacts for each member club. The Gujarati Muslim League is clearly well organised, and since its formation in 1995 has grown from 12 to 26 teams. Yet its existence is barely known beyond the tight-knit community in which its teams are based. Only three are members of the Club Cricket Conference, the organisation which has administered the grass-roots game for 83 years.

In contrast to the sparsely-attended end-of-season get-togethers run by avowedly more senior leagues, all the teams in the Gujarati Muslim League are represented. There must be more than 200 men in the room, the tables littered with empty Coca-Cola bottles and the appetising aroma of the meal to come wafting along the corridors. The guest speaker is Tony Banks, MP for Newham North-West and, at the time, Minister for Sport. When Banks demands that the England and Wales Cricket Board should trawl the inner cities and the ethnic minorities for talented players, the applause is loud, long and genuine. But it is also applause in recognition of the fact that a different kind of "establishment" has finally started to show interest.

There are numerous awards, including one for the best-kept ground. It is at this point that the difficulties faced by this fledgling league become starkly apparent. The winner is West Ham Park – a swathe of urban greenery a mere Shaka Hislop goal-kick away from the football ground, with a mosque at one corner and the crossed hammers of the West Ham badge daubed on many of the surrounding walls. Like most metropolitan parks, it was created in the late Victorian era from a private estate donated to the people of the neighbourhood. That neighbourhood is now almost entirely Asian; on Premiership matchdays its one-time white residents pour back. It is not especially ugly, but neither is it remotely attractive. It is simply the best that the league can find.

In "Anyone for Cricket?", an Asian club official talks of the ground his team plays on: "This is what we could afford, really." It has no sightscreens, there is litter on the outfield and, as the dressing rooms are a long walk away, the players tend to change behind trees on the edge of the field. "We played a white team at their ground last year. It was a really good, well-kept pitch. We had teas, the bar, the traditional sort of things but they didn't want to come here because it was not up to scratch for them. Too rough. They didn't want to injure their good heads."

IT IS NOT ONLY POOR FACILITIES that handicap Asian and black cricketers in the eyes of the "white establishment". The way in which these communities choose to play the game, what "Anyone for Cricket?" calls their "culture", is also markedly different.

This is one of the most fascinating sections of the report. First, the style of play. White players characterise Afro-Caribbeans as "flamboyant". They "tend to play their shots", and are "incredible athletes". Asian cricketers are "wristy and stylish", "shorter in stature" and "play nice shots off the back foot". Stereotypes, yes, but positive ones.

So how do the whites interviewed see themselves? "A little more cautious", "not quite so free-spirited", "more for building an innings". Typically English: self-effacing, reserved. How, then, are white cricketers viewed by black and Asian players? Ah, now we're getting some plain speaking. "Too boring and too slow", "very negative", "all front foot", "mechanically-built", "it's like they haven't got any natural ability", "they prefer the text book, that the shot should be correct". Harsh – but fair?

The divergence is even greater when it comes to the importance of competition. One white cricketer: "I play to win but I don't take it massively seriously. If I drop a catch or go for a few runs bowling, somebody has a go at me but I'm not worried, life's too short." Another: "It's the social banter during the game, it's the drink afterwards."

Black and Asian players: "If the game isn't competitive, how are you going to enjoy it?"

"When I ask for hard cricket I mean guys coming in at 90 miles an hour trying to do damage to you and you've got to be good enough to stay there and bat. In this country you don't get that."

"The Asians play cricket like the West Indians: they play to win, it's not a family or a friendly affair."

Fine. But there is a downside to this "win at all costs" mentality, and the comments of the umpires are revealing. One of the black umpires said: "You get more trouble with the Asian teams – all the time. I think they find it difficult to accept the decision of the umpire and they very easily accuse the umpire of bias ... You've got to be on the ball with the West Indians. A lot of white umpires don't like to umpire in West Indian matches, they can't handle it. It's very boisterous."

A white umpire who regularly stands in Asian cricket: "The biggest difference between the Essex County Leagues and the West

Indian and Asian leagues is the players' behaviour ... With white man's cricket only one or two of them will appeal but, with the Gujarati or the Sri Lankan League, nearly the whole team will appeal. They can be at square leg or point and they still appeal."

The black umpire probably gets closest to explaining why the "white establishment" views all-Asian teams with suspicion: "The Asians tend to be very temperamental. They basically want to win, they want to win at all costs and that causes a lot of friction. They don't play cricket to do anything else but win."

The issue, then, is whether one "culture" is more acceptable than another. The "white establishment" would no doubt highlight their game's fundamental decency, with moderately competitive cricket played with little aggravation, on good pitches in pleasant surroundings. Black and Asian cricketers would merely pull out a copy of the (admittedly unofficial) Test league table, and point to England's position at its foot.

THERE IS AN ASPECT of "white establishment" cricket which Asian clubs in particular struggle to come to terms with: the Sunday afternoon friendly. These are games played purely for pleasure, where the result is largely immaterial. Far more important is the enjoyment and physical exercise they give to cricketers who do not want the extra pressure that league matches invariably bring. The rules are well established: bat until you're dismissed or, if not, don't go too far past 200 before declaring. Give everyone a game. And if one side is clearly stronger than the other, do everything possible to spin things out until the bar opens.

After spending 16 years in one of the minor Essex county leagues, my own club switched to the Herts & Essex League last season. Its members are mostly villages on the border of the two counties, including some deliciously bucolic settings which might even please Michael Henderson. It is also an overwhelmingly "white" competition: the multi-ethnic composition of our 1st XI in particular is not the norm. Yet this has not brought out any of the negative attitudes which "Anyone for Cricket?" implied were latent within the Essex club scene.

On Sundays, we play friendlies only. While some clubs rush

"Want some more, you Paki bastards?" Six months later, he joined the police

headlong to create yet more leagues and marginalise the recreational cricketer, our members show no desire to add yet another layer of competition. As chairman (and a former employee of the Sports Council), I fully support this view: Sunday is when we uphold our commitment to "Sport for All". The age of our members ranges from eight to very nearly 80, and it's important that colts and veterans alike can play secure in the knowledge that they're not going to get their block knocked off by some psychopath in pursuit of maximum bowling points, or sledged by a jerk in wraparound shades who's seen the Aussies doing it and thinks it's perfectly appropriate for Little Snorescombe 4th XI.

As fixture secretary as well, I strive to apply the principle of "Sport For All" – which means arranging games against teams from other cultures. We're perfectly happy to adapt our teatime catering, cutting out the ham sandwiches and providing more vegetarian options. As for the reluctance of many Asian cricketers to stay behind after a game and socialise, a criticism made by several "white establishment" outfits in "Anyone for Cricket?", we're well aware that Muslims will not be quaffing pints until closing time and accept that beer sales might dip slightly on the day. Instead, we would hope that a few of our opponents might linger for a chat over a fruit juice or Coca-Cola. However, these are issues which "Anyone for Cricket?" presents in a somewhat biased manner, in its overall aim of trying to paint a picture of white discrimination. We hear plenty about Asian teams apparently failing to find fixtures because their players don't drink alcohol, and about requests for egg and tuna sandwiches being greeted with the retort: "Well, is it a Paki side?". And not enough about clubs which, as one secretary stated, believe that "cricket is for cricketers, no matter what colour or creed".

When clubs are compelled to play each other not by choice but because they are in the same league, then many of these delicate negotiations are destroyed by petty, tit-for-tat behaviour which transcends mere racial barriers. They didn't stay for a drink with you, so you won't hang around at their place. Their sandwiches were curling at the dges, so you won't bother giving them that extra box of cakes. The Sunday friendly, in contrast, relies on collusion – the tacit understanding between two fixture secretaries and 22 players that the match has been created for the purpose of pleasure and recreation. But it doesn't always work out like that.

Take one new game last season, against an Asian side based in Ilford which does not play in the Gujarati Muslim League. Since our Sunday line-ups are a motley combination of old pros, colts and drinkers, I arranged a 2nd XI fixture at their place, at what the Club Cricket Conference grading system terms "weak-medium".

During the week leading up to the match, our opponents phoned to say that the pavilion at the ground they use had burned down. Arson, they suspected. I sympathised, and was delighted when they said that, rather than cancelling, they would try to find an alternative venue. This they did – one of east London's less salubrious parks. When they phoned again a day later to announce that they had deemed the park unacceptable and had instead booked a pitch at one of the area's best company sports grounds, their approval rating zoomed into the stratosphere.

Matchday came and, sadly, their approval rating zoomed back down again. They asked to play "overs" rather than "declaration", a format which eliminates the draw and guarantees a result. OK, we said: their ground, their playing conditions. They then fielded three genuine quicks, and played the game like it was a high-intensity international. It was a classic example of cross-cultural misunderstanding; of the "win at all costs" mentality destroying what could otherwise have been a pleasant afternoon.

We only lost by 20-odd runs, but the damage had been done. When it came to reviewing fixtures at a recent committee meeting and deciding which were not worth keeping, this one was top of the list. This means that, despite all our opponents' hard work in the run-up to the match, I will need to tell them that we do not wish to renew. Even if they were to convince me that things would be different next year, I know – because our captain told me – that if the game were to appear on the card for 2000, none of our members who played in the first encounter would make themselves available. This is not because they are prejudiced: it is simply because they do not want to play this type of cricket. Typical English softies? Maybe so. But it's their Sunday afternoon.

THE BERTIE JOEL CUP is a prestigious midweek knockout competition, founded in 1967. Bertie himself was an indefatigable founder of cricket teams and supporter of good causes in the London area. If you asked him nicely, or so it was said, he could get you membership of MCC inside the week. Entry is by invitation, and black and Asian clubs have always featured on the list. This year's competition was won by Lambeth Enterprise, a West Indian community club which plays on a modest recreation ground in Wimbledon. They beat South Woodford, an old "white establishment" club from Essex who nonetheless fielded seven Asian players in the final. It was a match conducted in an excellent spirit, a perfect illustration of how cricket can spread the message of multi-racial harmony.

Last year, another Essex club reached the final – although the circumstances were rather more controversial. An all-Asian outfit from one of the county's minor leagues saw off a succession of senior rivals. However, each round brought grumbles from the defeated club that the victors had drafted in "ringers" who were not bona fide club members. Stories circulated about players changing in the wrong dressing room, unsure of who their team-mates actually were; of players known to be professionals elsewhere turning out for the Asian club.

The matter reached a head when a top Surrey side were beaten by a lineup which included the sometime Pakistan captain and wicketkeeper Rashid Latif. The losers lodged a complaint, based on information that Latif was not a club member: "It was freely admitted in the bar afterwards that he just happened to know one of the members of their team." However, the circumstances of Latif's appearance were utterly bizarre. According to one of the Surrey club's officials: "He opened the batting and scored 70-odd in quick time, posed for pictures at teatime (not normal behaviour for a regular player or club member), then bowled his overs off the reel, shook everyone's hands and left the field! I think our captain was a bit baffled by all this and did not object to them bringing on a 12th man."

When questioned, the Asian club admitted that this had been Latif's only appearance for them all year. Yet they produced "evidence" – a faxed copy of a subscription form – apparently confirming that he had paid his £50 membership fee, in cash.

For the organisers of the Bertie Joel Cup, unused to dealing with matters of such sensitivity, there was an obvious danger: to kick the Asian club out of the competition would inevitably lead to an accusation of racial prejudice. In the end, the "evidence" had to be accepted as there was no further way to prove whether Rashid Latif was a club member or not. But the affair led to the final being conducted in a discordant atmosphere. There had been more wrangles about the Asian team's win in the semi-final, this time to do with the standard of umpiring. And, quite by chance, it was the club they had just beaten who were staging the final – and whose members turned out in force to cheer on their opponents. The Asian team then refused to eat the host club's lunch, and remained in their dressing room throughout the interval.

These unsavoury events discoloured what would otherwise have been remembered as an example of club cricket at its finest. The match went to the very last ball, when the Asian side were beaten only by virtue of having lost more wickets in a thrilling scores-level tie. It was, however, the outcome that the Bertie Joel Cup committee were hoping for. It would have been very difficult to tell the defending champions that they were not being invited to participate again.

TOWARDS THE END of "Anyone for Cricket?", all the respondents were asked what could be done to make cricket in Essex more integrated. The answers ranged from the general – "They have to calm down a bit, they have to let us in, have to let us play, have to give us space" – to the very specific: "Don't have criteria where you got to have four youngsters' [colts] teams before you join a white man's league – this is rubbish. Proper wickets should be provided all round, not just for the white teams."

The latter comment is heartfelt, but idealistic. Most of those clubs with "proper wickets" have them simply due to the happenstance of being founded 100 or more years ago. As for who exactly should be providing these "proper wickets", I doubt that too many local councils would rank cricket above healthcare, education and crime prevention on their list of priorities.

The question of criteria for gaining admission to the "white man's league" is more complex since, at the top level, this is now a matter for the ECB. It is ironic that, at the same time as the ECB has formed a Racism Study Group in conjunction with the Commission for Racial Equality and Sport England (formerly the Sports Council), and is working to increase participation rates among the black and Asian population, the creation of Premier Leagues at the apex of a pyramid system makes it even more unlikely that clubs from ethnic minorities will reach the highest levels. Junior coaching schemes, sightscreens, covers and all the other accoutrements of the "white establishment" are now deemed necessary to make progress. So what about those 11 keen and gifted black guys playing in a parks league? Sorry, lads: where's your structured development programme?

A FEW MONTHS AGO, you would have found Ronnie Irani batting with a tree for stumps in West Ham Park – and thoroughly enjoying the experience. The Essex and England all-rounder was helping to publicise an annual cricket course for some 200 youngsters from the London Borough of Newham. He told those taking part that it was the aim of the county to produce a professional player from the scheme. "If you drew a matrix through the number of kids who wanted to play and the area with the fewest opportunities, you would be looking at Newham," added Mike Boyers, Essex's development manager, while pointing out that 40 per cent of the county's age-group squads are from ethnic minority backgrounds.

This sort of work not only refutes the allegations made in "Anyone for Cricket?" that Essex is the home of unequal opportunities. It also chimes with the ECB's commitment to anti-racist policies, and echoes what is going on elsewhere in the capital. The Middlesex Cricket Board, for example, has helped to create a junior club in Victoria Park, Hackney – another area with a large non-white population. And the London Community Cricket Association has staged two six-a-side tournaments under the banner of the Hit Racism for Six campaign, attracting teams from a wide range of cultural backgrounds.

Meanwhile, in June this year, Hit Racism for Six made a formal submission to the ECB's Racism Study Group. They urged that the ECB should draw up a development plan for the inner cities, with special reference to black and Asian cricket – something omitted from the *Raising the Standard* blueprint. "To make equal opportunities a reality and not just a slogan," the group declared. "The ECB will have to invest in the infrastructure of the game in the inner cities."

None of this stuff would ever impress Terry the beamer bowler – wherever he is. His likes are beyond redemption. However, Essex, supposedly the county of cricketing apartheid, is now working with the Gujarati Muslim League to create what Mike Boyers calls "a pathway of opportunity" for the youngsters on the Newham course. This does not mean cherry-picking the best and packing them off to a small band of elite clubs. Almost the opposite, in fact: it means recognising that some black and Asian cricketers wish to play the game within their own social and religious groupings, and providing decent facilities for them to do so. The League and the Essex Cricket Association are putting together a joint Lottery bid with the aim of creating two high-quality pitches on the open spaces of Wanstead Flats, just a mile from the very heart of London's Asian community.

From West Ham Park to Wanstead Flats: less than an inch separates them on the A-Z, yet it's a tricky two-bus journey. For the black and Asian cricketers of Essex and east London, the symbolism could not be more appropriate. ☽

THE WINNER, AND NEW CHAMPION OF THE WORLD SHANE WARNE
DISPOSES OF MOIN KHAN, SETTLING THE DESTINY OF THE TROPHY, LORD'S

WHAT A LOAD OF COBBERS MCC MEMBERS RESERVE THEIR RIGHT OF APPROVAL AS AUSTRALIA REJOICE

Simon Hattenstone

Me and Hicky

Simon Hattenstone is a features writer for the *Guardian*. In 1997 he was shortlisted for Interview of the Year at the UK press awards. His book, *Out Of It*, is published by Sceptre and is currently being turned into a film.

Wickedest wicket I was going to choose any wicket by Michael Holding – the sensuality of his run-up was enough to turn any straight man gay. But in the end I have to opt for Warne v Gatting. Every time you see it again you try to play it, anticipate it, but you never can.

Soundest bite "The bowler's Holding, the batsman's Willey." (Brian Johnston, circa 1980)

For many years I used to play a game as I walked home from school, from university, from work. Walking was so tedious, and this helped pass the time. I called it Road Cricket. It was very simple to play: you selected an England cricket team and an opposition, and then counted your steps. If a car passed, your player would be out, and you were on to the next batsman. So if three cars passed in rapid succession, you may find you had lost Gooch, Atherton and Lamb for, say, two. If you were on a quiet road late at night you may find Gooch beating his 334 against India. Whenever I tried to explain the game to friends they thought I was bonkers, obsessive. But don't you see, I would wail, you could make the walk home so much more enjoyable, so much more competitive.

There was only one time I would cheat at Road Cricket: when Graeme Hick was batting. Even though this was well before the Zimbawean qualified to play for England, he was always in my team. and he always scored a pack of runs. If a car passed and he was out, I would pretend that the announcer had named the wrong batsman, or that he'd crossed and Gatting was out instead, or that it was a no-ball. I just couldn't face the possibility of Hick failing, so he dutifully scored hundred after hundred after hundred. His average was 151 – not that far off his county average. And when I gave him the captaincy it rocketed to around 202. Unprecedented.

I was fixated with Graeme Hick. Still am, actually. The strange thing is I am not cricket mad. Yes, I know the names of the top players and have an inkling of their averages, but I have never played the game, never attended cricket matches, don't have a clue about the difference between mid-on and and silly far out. But Graeme Hick was a different matter.

It started in 1984 when he made his championship debut for Worcestershire (82 not out in the last game against Surrey, from the depths of no.9). I scanned the sports pages and as the years passed summer days seemed to be headlined with ever-increasing greed by this tanned country boy with the pleasantly anodyne features. He couldn't stop scoring runs, breaking records. He was the youngest player to score 2,000 in a season. His 50th first-class century was notched up before he was 25 – even younger than Bradman (who'd played far fewer innings at that age, admittedly). In the final game of his annus mirabilis, 1988, Worcestershire had to acquire maximum batting points against Glamorgan to keep Kent at bay and clinch the championship; Hicky guided them home with 17 balls to spare then rendered all calculations redundant by setting up an innings win with 197, a county-record-equalling 10th hundred of the season, undaunted by the petroleum jelly and engine oil spread over the New Road pitch by some would-be saboteur with a penchant for Kent. The next year another classic innings against Somerset took Worcestershire to the title. When the heat was on, Hick took over the kitchen. Or something like that.

Then there was Taunton, May 1988, when he strode to 405, the highest score made in England this century. Hick was 21. The club chairman Duncan Fearnley said he was twice the player the legendary New Zealand and Worcestershire stalwart Glenn Turner had been at the same age. In the same month, now 22, he joined the immortals by claiming 1,000 runs before May was out. Only six players had previously achieved this. He did it in 11 innings, two more than Bradman; Turner had done it in 18. Michael Henderson wrote in the *Guardian*: "It recalled Pinter's judgment of Len Hutton that his bat was part of his nervous system ... It puts him at the age of 22 years and five days among the game's truly great. So much so soon: how much can this young man deliver?" In the same paper Frank Keating declared the "blushingly boyish Hicky ... worthy to take his place among the May-time heroes". According to the

Observer, Hicky was "destined to become the greatest player in the world, the new Bradman".

Dear Graeme Hick
I am a journalist and book writer. I am not the world's most knowledgeable cricket fan, but for years I have been a great fan of yours, fascinated by your career and a close follower of your averages for both Worcester and England. I have been asked whether I would write a piece about you for the cricket book The New Ball Volume 3. I hope you agree to be interviewed for the piece.
All the best
Simon Hattenstone

It is a dream come true. I have been asked to interview Graeme Hick. I want to tell him that I love him, and would defend him to the end of the earth, but it may put him off so I opt for English restraint, with a smidge of fandom. I am desperate for the reponse, tear open my mail every day, scan the postmark desperately for Worcester. I have interviewed many big names over the years – Woody Allen, Henry Kissinger, Steven Spielberg. But no one's excited me like Hick. I'm tingling at the prospect. It's embarrassing.

Still nothing in the post. But he probably wants to make a considered response, work out where exactly the interview should take place, make me feel comfy. Hicky's considerate like that.

IT WAS IN 1991 that Hicky fever peaked. Not just for me, but for everyone – even the cynics and professionals who actually understood cricket. After his seven-year wait, he finally qualified for the England team – and automatic selection, of course. He was going to save us from mediocrity and worse. A nation waited.

His autiobiography was already published but Hicky wasn't flash or daft or self-destructive; he was just a farmboy who loved to clout a cricket ball through the skies. The nearest he had come to excess was when he went out and drank a couple of bottles of wine with his parents to celebrate his 405.

He was unnerved by the expectation. "If you are enjoying your life, you enjoy your cricket. They seem to go together. It's amazing how easy it is to go out and play a game if you are happy within yourself," he told Brough Scott in the *Independent on Sunday*. But Scott himself sounded a portentous note. "Just at this moment the promise is so fresh and so infinite that there is also a touch of sadness about it," he wrote on the eve of Hick's Test debut. "The evening sun was glinting on new leaves everywhere. Not all of them will grow through to perfection. Graeme Hick is being burdened with quite unreasonable, simplistic hype ..."

Peter Roebuck, writing in the *Sunday Times*, said there was a chance Hick would fail, but it wouldn't be nerves that let him down. "His technique is too sound, his shot production too precise and his vision too sharp for him to allow pressure to dictate terms. If he loses his way, it is because of mechanical failure, for Hick is a rigid batsman, an apostle of heavy bats and clean swings." Perhaps, he added, his height could work against him when confronting the world's great pacemen. But he was just being controversial, doing what journalists were paid to do.

THE MORE I DISCOVERED about Hick the more inextricably linked we became. He had asthma and meningitis as a child. I had had asthma and encephalitis as a child. It wasn't so much a coincidence, it was a phenomenon. We both understood suffering and alienation, Hicky and me. I imagined him and me, as children, desperate in the dark, locked out, blinded by headaches.

I waited for the big day. His Test debut. It finally came: Headingley, June 6. On the way home the previous evening I'd played Road Cricket past exhaustion. Hick batted no.1 to no.11. When I got home, I walked back to the tube station in an attempt to beat his 405. However much I cheated, it didn't work. His top score, batting at 11, was 391. Many great sportsmen get butterflies. It has been said that without nerves you are doomed. I remember reading how the great Arsenal forward Charlie George, famously insouciant laddish Charlie George, used to vomit before each match.

I don't know how Graeme was feeling, but I had the runs, butterflies, nausea. I tried the sensible approach – good night's sleep, pasta, light exercise, warm-ups – but I couldn't beat my nerves. My girlfriend asked what was wrong. I told her Hicky was making his début tomorrow, and she didn't seem to hear. She asked if I had hiccups. I tried to meditate the evening away. When I couldn't sleep, I tried to meditate the night away. Nothing. Just stomach cramps.

I was up for 6.30am. Actually, I'd not slept. But I still felt fresh, strong, resolute. Today history was was to be made. Year Zero, the great English revival starts here. We were entering the golden age of Graeme Hick. The man Ian Botham nicknamed God. Phil Neale, his county captain, compared him to the great Liverpool team of the Eighties: "So technically correct it's a bit like a machine." The *Today* newspaper anticipated the great day. "He is now in a position to dominate cricket well into the next century and is carrying the same torch that Bradman and Richards have held before him." The series was not England v West Indies; it was Hicky v West Indies.

He came, he saw, he didn't conquer. The early signs, admittedly, had been rather promising. In the opening one-dayer at Edgbaston he'd made 14, in the second a presentable 29, followed by a matchwinning unbeaten 86 as England swept the Texacos at Lord's. Come Headingley, however, while the other Graham, Goochie, was driving England to their first Test win over the Windies since *Seasons in the Sun* was No.1 with arguably his finest innings, Hicky – caught chasing one from Courtney and bat-padded by Malcolm – managed a pair of half-dozens. Ducks followed at Lord's and Trent Bridge and by August he'd been dropped, having mustered 75 runs at 10.71. I was distraught.

Mediocre in New Zealand that winter, he was dropped again the following August, having passed 50 (and barely so at that, making 51 against Pakistan) just once in 11 Tests and 17 innings. New Zealand's John Bracewell dismissed him as a flat-track bully, who panicked at the first hint of pace or guile. He was demoted to no.7 in the order. It was humiliating, I couldn't begin to explain what had gone wrong. My stomach was wrenched in permanent knots. Each innings was tougher than the last. For both of us.

But 17 innings, I told myself, pah, 17 innings, barely the embryo of a Test career. All the batting greats took their time to make a mark in the national side. Well, some of them – Amiss and Gatting and Gooch. Gooch barely scored a run for England before his early 30s. And there he was, all gritted teeth and bulldog pride, Mr England.

The critics began to crucify Hick – many of the same people who had eulogised him only a few months earlier. They were revelling in his failure. The tabloids called in psychologists. Dr Ian Cockerell of the sports science department of Birmingham University said Hick exemplified "catastrophe theory". If a player wants to win and is aroused or psyched up for the game, that's great. But if he is over-aroused, psyched out, he overprepares, and is paralysed by by self-doubt. And this, they claimed was the fate of Graeme Hick.

And there was the fact that he was socially ill at ease. There was Bumpy and Lucky and Lugsy in the Worcester changing room, but Hicky was just Graeme Hick, the good old run machine. In rare confessional mode he said: "I've got no nickname. I'm pretty drab and I've never done anything stupid enough to earn one." You could hear the twinge of regret in his voice.

He tried to explain himself: "Because I don't show much emotion, I'm misread. I want to do as well as the person next to me." The experts assaulted his weaknesses. Not only was he dull, they decided he wasn't even an interesting cricketer. Whereas Gower had class and Botham had heart and Jack Russell had impudence and Gooch had that magnificient grit, Hick just had his fatal flaw – his mental weakness. And at his strongest, they said, what did he do but crudely crash the ball through the air with ox-like strength. In one of the most beautiful and damning assessments, Roebuck wrote: "Hick has no personality ... [his] anonymity is not a fault so much as as a fact, a fact that limits his appeal. This is not a fearless explorer, just a settler, a peaceable organised man whose horizons are narrow, a middle-ranking officer who just looks like Alexander the Great ... it's hard to think of a great sportsman, or a great man, so indistinct. Hardly a wrinkle or chipped tooth can be detected in Hick, nothing on which spectators can seize and say 'So this is our man'. He seems like an unfished sculpture, perfectly formed and yet somehow empty." Bastard. Bastard, bastard, bastard. BASTARD. This is my Graeme you're rubbishing. My present, my future, my hopes. Bastard.

THE STRANGE THING is that Hick did start to perform at Test level. By 1995 he had averaged 40-something in his last 22, and overall he was well into the late-middle 30s. There'd been tons in

South Africa and India – albeit neither in winning causes. He was promising to dominate as he had done for Worcestershire. But still neither the commentators nor selectors were happy. Whatever he did was not enough. Every time he thought he'd made his point, secured his future, he would be dropped. It didn't matter that he was performing at a higher level than most of the squad: he had betrayed his promise. So he went.

Hicky's relative failure became a microcosm of the English game – all that was wrong with it, and all it had aspired to. Eternal hope turned to eternal disappointment. Critics regarded his Test form as an act of bad faith. They had not only believed in him, they had promised us that he would do it for England. They had staked their expertise on his success, and lost. His failure was their failure. Even if he had been averaging the magical 40, the mark of a quality batsman, it would still not have been good enough because it was not the Hutton let alone the Bradman they had promised.

His relative failure also rammed home another ghastly home truth – that the British game, the very game these experts spent their days trailing and tagging, was second rate, third rate even. And Hick proved it conclusively. The genius of the county circuit couldn't climb the next rung. True, his average was way ahead of Crawley and Ramprakash and Butcher and any number of near-England regulars. But it didn't matter. The experts' bitterness soon turned to bile. They decided Hicky failed because he didn't want to succeed sufficiently. He didn't understand what it meant to fight for Saint George. He wasn't one of us, not a true Brit. Still Zimbabwean at heart. Even among the England squad there seemed to be a collective urge for him to implode.

Hicky no longer looked the rosy-cheeked country boy of his youth. He had been forced to confront his own fallibility. In 1993 he had said: "After a while you get tired of being laughed at. I am not someone who enjoys losing or failing." On the occasions he wasn't dropped, he limped out to bat, once brave shoulders hunched, helmet bowed, defeated.

They were terrible years for Hicky and me. I became as withdrawn as he did. Sometimes my friends and I would be in the pub, drinking away, laughing carelessly, enjoying our own company. And then the subject would turn to cricket. I always knew what was coming next. "What the bleedin' hell has happened to Graeme Hick?" "What a tosser – pathetic, little squib of a player. Panicker." "Your man's turned out a right loser, hey Si?" If I could sense the conversation turning to Hicky, I would rush to the loo, or offer to get another round in. Anything but face the music. My arguments were sound – 100 centuries, youngest player to do this, that and everything, dropped every other game, look at Goochie – but I knew my blush would give me away. Perhaps in my heart I'd become a doubter. Perhaps I myself didn't have the strength, the mental fibre, to stand up to the onslaught.

Three weeks have passed since my first letter to Hicky. No reply. Nor to my two follow-ups. I assume there must have been a hiccup, no pun intended, with the post. In the following letters I tell Graeme I know there must have been a cock-up in the post. I have phoned up New Road most days. The woman at the end of the phone knows me now. For the first week she would ask, honest as you like, what my name was and what I wanted. She always seemed to be on the verge of calling "Graaaemmmmme, phone for you. Must be a friend." When I said it was Simon from *The New Ball* she would gulp and say Graeme wasn't available.

I think I am becoming a little paranoid. Week two and she doesn't seem quite as friendly. Week three, she's re-establishing intimacy, but it's a different kind of intimacy. Almost motherly. "Simon, love," she says a few weeks into our relationship, "d'you ever get the feeling that Graeme doesn't want to talk to you?"

Dear Graeme Hick
I know you have not replied to any of my letters or calls, but I am still a great admirer of yours. I will be coming down to the next Worcester home match, and will be doing my piece about you by talking to fans etc. Of course, the piece would be much better if you agreed to speak to me – or at least reply to me. But whatever, so be it. I enclose an article I recently wrote about Alex Ferguson to show you you have little to be scared of.
All the best
Simon Hattenstone

No one likes him, friends would **taunt** me; they don't even have a **nickname** for him in the dressing room

Perhaps the most hurtful accusation was that Hick could never be a true cricketing legend because he was boring, stupid, a dullard, a social misfit. No one likes him, my friends would taunt me; they don't even have a nickname for him in the dressing room at Worcester.

The determination of Hick to triumph over the collective will was astonishing. Every year he was dropped, every year he came back mid-series and proved the doubters wrong (but not sufficiently wrong, clearly) until he was dropped again. Every year he tended to give one interview at the beginning of each season in which he would reveal how he'd beaten the demons. Finally. In 1995, he said he'd recovered his self-confidence thanks to the help of a sports psychologist: "Suddenly there was this person who actually thought there was some good in me. I think I needed that. He cleared my mind of all the bad things. I admit I was temperamentally suspect."

His average was rising onwards and upwards, to no avail. In Sydney the previous winter, Mike Atherton declared with Hick 98 not out against Australia: possibly the cruellest act of captaincy in cricket history. Atherton, who subsequently confessed his grave error, told the world Hick had been scoring too slowly. The press called for him to be dropped. After scoring 98 not out against Australia!

The pattern repeated itself again and again. Runs, one bad innings, one more defeat, and dropped. In 1998 Alan Lee wrote in the *Times* that there "had never been a cricketer who has been so loudly touted then so publicly scorned". Meanwhile, Hicky told the world, he'd regained his confidence again and this time it was for good. Indeed, he was so sure of himself that he could talk about how he had almost been destroyed. He told Lee: "I took all the comments and criticism personally, whereas I realise now that it's just how the system works and that the same thing will happen to others. I was so insecure that I wouldn't talk to people I didn't know and I'd sometimes avert my eyes from those I did. My self-esteem was very low. I didn't walk into a place and stand broad-shouldered with my head high. I would now. I had some demons for sure."

And sure enough, soon after, he was dropped for the tour to Australia. And sure enough he was recalled when the annual injury round hit hard. Hick was magnificent in Australia. Batting at an insulting no. 7 he scored 68 in thirtysomething balls in his first innings at Perth, and went on to play a crucial pair of innings in a low-scoring match to snatch victory by 12 runs in Melbourne – 39 and 60. I remember lying with the radio to my pillow pleading for the one extra run that would take his average for the match to 50, and series to 40. It never came. The Tests were followed by a heroic and unequalled run of form in the one-dayers – three centuries on the trot. That was barely eight months ago.

He came back, began the World Cup imperiously then subsided like everyone else against South Africa and India. Immediately after England were eliminated at Edgbaston he incurred the wrath of the press (and team-mates) by asking colleagues to sign some t-shirts he could sell for his benefit year rather than sharing in a session of Maoist self-criticism. But any Hick loyalist knows he has always preferred to keep his grief to himself.

He was then dropped for the Tests against New Zealand. Inexplicable and unsurprising. The recall came when Nasser Hussain broke a finger at Lord's – he was given lbw for 11 in the first innings at Old Trafford, and even the Hick baiters agreed he wasn't out. He never got a chance to bat in the second. After the match, he was dropped for the rest of the season. Then he was dropped for the tour to South Africa, against whom he has scored two thunderous centuries. Doubtless be recalled in time for the second Test ...

IT'S SIX WEEKS since my first letter. I have heard nothing. Not an even a terse no. I never thought I'd say this, but I have to admit I feel a little annoyed with Hicky. If he treats me like this, how does he treat his enemies? I am beginning to suspect that my worst fears about his personality – a little boorish and thoughtless – were well-founded. I know he needs to spend time with his two children, and it is his benefit year, but Graeme ... give a sucker a break.

Dear Graeme Hick
Surprise, surprise, no response to my interview request. I tried my best – lovely cuttings in the post, repeated reminders about what a hero you are for me – but still nothing. Have I done something to hurt

you? Do you think I may feel let down on meeting my hero. Well, I
assure you I won't be. So, one final attempt – after your two hundreds
last week you are more elevated in the cricket pantheon than ever.
This could be the piece that wins you back your Test place. I know I
should hate your cowardice for failing to reply to the press, that I
should despise your ignorance for not answering a true supporter,
but I don't. I am still one of your greatest fans. So, please, please, please
grant me an interview. I will be coming to Worcestershire on
Wednesday to watch you score another century.
All the best
Simon Hattenstone

Aficionados say New Road is one of the most beautiful grounds
in the country – small, intimate and curtained in churches, spires
and the cathedral. It's a perfect day. The last day of summer, and
the last match of the season. Worcestershire v Middlesex. When I
arrive, Hicky is settling in. The score is 80 for two, Hicky 17 not
out. After a 16-year wait I finally get to see him in the flesh. I'm only
here for the day, but if he's in 405 not out mode, of course, I can
always arrange a sleepover. He hits his first shot for two runs. The
thin crowd whistles. "Ooh he didn't play that well. It's like one of
my snooker shots," says an elderly gentleman to his elderly
gentlemen friends. "He's looking a bit ropey today, isn't he?" Next
ball, he pads away. He takes a quick, indecisive single. He flaps at
a half-decent ball by Gus Fraser. Hick is out – he's lasted five minutes
since I arrived, scored three runs. Vikram Solanki is batting next.
He goes on to score 150-odd. I go to the players' balcony looking
for Hick. All the players are there, except for Hick. I have a nasty
feeling he is avoiding me. Perhaps he thinks I am stalking him. A man,
the coach I think, asks me what I want. I tell him I would like an
autograph. He says, rather brutally, that I should come back later.
I wander round the ground looking for Hicky buffs. I tell the man
at the burger bar that I've come all the way from London to watch
him play and he scored three runs while I was here. "It's typical
Graeme Hick, that is. If you hadn't come, he'd have a century no
trouble. That'll be £2.10."

Mr and Mrs Woodcock seem to have a quarter of the ground to

themselves and their blankets. They look as if they have been following Worcestershire for half a century. "Oh no, no, no," says Mr Woodcock, "I'm a Lancashire man through and through. We've only been coming here eight years." But he must be a Hick fan by now? "Not really," says Mr Woodcock. "The number of times he gets out in his mid-teens is criminal. His legside play is terrible – he gets more leg-byes than runs on the leg side." Mrs Woodcock says he seems a lovely man, the boy next door. "But he'll never be one of the greats. Not dedicated enough. I'm surprised you've not compared him to Geoff," she says to Mr Woodcock. "Oh no," says Mr Woodcock, appalled at the heresy. "I would never compare him to Geoff. He can't take pace, can't play off his back foot, hasn't got the right stuff in the head." I make my excuses and leave.

It takes a while, but eventually I find my kindred spirits. Joan Evans turns to John Evans. "He's the best in the world isn't he, our Graeme?" "O yessssss," says John Evans. "Best in the world – but to be fair he was even better when he was a kid – between 17 and 23. Mind you he never got a fair crack of the whip did he? The papers buggered it up for him. I tell you what if he was from Surrey, or Lancashire even, he would never have been dropped." "That's right," says Joan Evans. "It's a case of your face fitting." This is what I'm after – a wholly biased eulogy of my man. "The thing is every time he gets picked now the pressure is greater. I tell you what though ... it was great seeing him score his hundredth hundred. Wouldn't have missed it for the world. Two centuries in the one match." When he reached the great landmark, the first people he ran to hug were his children. In the 1999 *Wisden* Roebuck attached great significance to it. He said it showed where his loyalties now lie.

Norman Homer says he has been coming to Worcester for 50-plus years. Hick, he says, is one of the best, the very best. How could they drop him after that one-innings recall, and a dodgy decision? He pulls his cheeks in and whistles at the madness. "Mind you, he's had plenty of chances. You have to say he's had plenty of chances. He's a brilliant fielder, he can bowl, if they fetched him to South Africa I think he would be man of the series. I do – man of the series. You ask Allan Donald if he's pleased that he won't be in South Africa. He'll be rubbing his hands, I promise you." Norman tells me how he got up at four in the morning to watch Hicky's first century against India on the television. I tell him I was there too – only with the radio. I'm beginning to feel an affinity with Norman Homer. I wonder whether I should tell him about how he hasn't responded to my approaches, how upset I am, but in the end I think it would be a betrayal of both Hick and Mr Homer.

Instead we talk about the conspiracy to undermine Hick. Mr Homer recalls the time Atherton declared with Hick on 98. "I spluttered when they started saying he should never play for England again because he'd scored 98 not out, too slowly. Can you believe that? I thought I was going to go under."

I'M WALKING round the outside of the ground where the players' cars are parked. Cricketers still struggle for their money, so if a company offers a sponsored car of course they will accept. In huge bold letters the sponsor and the sponsored are printed. "Vikram Solanki sponsored by Silver Life" on a silver Merc, "David Leatherdale – David Price Motors" on his Peugeot and poor Stuart Lampitt's people carrier sponsored by Walker Renault. It is amazing how people will invade their own privacy. How could a cricketer complain about being approached by the general public when driving one of these monstrosities?

On the way round, I see my *Guardian* colleague, the great cricket writer and *Wisden* editor Matthew Engel. I tell him I'm here to praise Graeme Hick, even though he's let me down. Engel gives me a look that suggests I'm a sad, deluded soul. "I wouldn't have him in my Test side," he says. Look at his average, though? And getting better all the time. "Yes," Engel says, " but look at the quality of the runs. He never scores when it matters. At Perth, when he made that 60 after coming out as a replacement, the match was dead. Even when he made that hundred against South Africa it rained for the next three and a half days so it had no consequence." Engel tells me they used to say Dean Jones and Zaheer Abbas were similar – they never scored when it mattered. "Compare Hick to the runs made by Atherton or Stewart. Particularly Atherton. When he makes runs, they always count. The number of matches Atherton has saved or won with his runs is phenomenal." I know Engel has a point. A bloody good point actually. But it would be crazy to concede it. Anyway, there is the future.

It's early afternoon, the sun is blazing unadulterated happiness, the skies are blue. I know there won't be another day like it this year. Nor another opportunity. I walk up to the players' balcony, see Hick and walk past. I walk back, and past again. Then I call to him, timidly. "Graeme? Graeme," I beseech. "Please could I have your autograph."

"Pass me your book," he says tersely. He scrawls a signature. No chance of a "Dear Simon" then, let alone "Dear Simon, my greatest my most resolute fan."

Graeme, I say, I've been writing to you for a long time. And phoning. I'm a journalist writing for a little publication called *The New Ball* and I am desperate to interview you. I'm not a great cricket fan, but I've always always been in ..." For a moment I think I'm going to say I've always been in love with you, but of course I haven't. Not really.

And it would only put him off. "I've always been a massive fan, Graeme. My name is Simon ..."

"New Ball?" He says sharply. "Nah, don't know it. Doesn't ring a bell ..."

I feel relieved. Graeme obviously didn't get the letters or phone calls. That's why he hasn't responded. It's just been a misunderstanding, and we're going to right it this second.

"Hey, what did you say your name was?"

"Simon."

"Simon?"

"Yes, Simon. Yes, please Graeme, Simon."

"I thought you wrote for the *Guardian*."

Oh Jesus! I realise I must have been writing to him on *Guardian* headed paper.

"Well I do work for the *Guardian*, but this is just an incy wincy cricket-loving book. So please – the interview?"

"I don't really fancy doing it. I'm just letting the waters settle. I'm not doing anything for a while."

"But I've come hundreds of miles ..."

"No. Sorry mate. No."

He turns away, with a grin. I think he's laughing at me. 🌑

Coming Attractions

The New Ball Volume 4
Heaven's XI *Published May 2000*

The next edition of *The New Ball* will be a one-off tribute to the players who have done most to enrich our lives, as voted for in our exclusive poll by readers, writers and yer odd actual cricketer. Each member of our heavenly lineup will be profiled by a similarly celestial array of scribblers. Contributors (at time of going to press) to include: **Frank Keating, David Frith, David Foot, Peter Roebuck, Mike Marqusee, Mike Coward, Robert Winder, Trevor Chesterfield, Rob Kitson** and **Alastair McLellan**.

If you would like to receive advance notification of future editions of *The New Ball*, please write to Sports Books Direct, 3 Luke Street, London EC2A 4PX